Diana Lampe's

Embroidered Pansies

WRITING ON STONE

Acknowledgements

Thank you to the following people for the part they have played in making this book happen, either directly or indirectly. It has been a heartwarming experience for me, to receive so much help and encouragement.

Charlotte, Sophie and Nicholas Harper, for being there

David Lampe, other family members and good friends, for love and support

Steph Litchfield, for looking after me

Geoffrey Brooks, for kindness and help

Krystyna and Bruno Koltun, for being so caring on the home front

Elisabeth Rundle, for keeping the home fires burning

Cheryl Armstrong, Writing on Stone, for believing in and publishing this book

Sally Milner, for cheerfully and patiently making it happen

Amanda Knobel, Paper Monkey, for the stunning book design

Andrew Sikorski, Art Atelier, for the beautiful photographs

Marion Trezise, for the gorgeous tea-cosies

Robin Errey, for the lovely hand-drawn tassel and stitch illustrations

Antoinette Stojadinovic, for framing my embroideries in such a complementary way

The Pansy Group, for friendship and so many other things: Cheryl Armstrong, Pam Arnott, Jenny Bradford, Jenny Brennan, Rita Crawford, Allyson Hamilton, Jan Jolliffe, Tiina Johnston, Dianne Smith, Judy Spence, Maggie Taylor and Marion Trezise

Dr Michael Pidcock, and the medical, nursing and scientific staff at the Haematology and Oncology Department at The Canberra Hospital, for special care and for giving me more time

A percentage of my royalties from this book will go to the Haematology Research Fund at The Canberra Hospital.

Diana Lampe 2005

For Charlotte, Sophie and Nicholas
I couldn't have hoped for more

First published in 2005 by
Writing on Stone
Australian Heritage Village
Cnr Antill Street and Federal Highway
Watson ACT 2602

© Diana Lampe, 2005
© Crochet patterns and designs,
Marion Tresize, 2005

Project Management by
Sally Milner
Photography by Andrew Sikorski,
Art Atelier, Canberra
Design by Amanda Knobel,
Paper Monkey, Canberra

Printed and bound in China

ISBN 1 876808 01 2

Contents

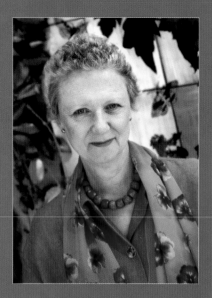

Introduction

There's rosemary, that's for remembrance;
pray you, love, remember.
and there is pansies, that's for thoughts
Shakespeare *Hamlet*

I have always just loved pansies, they are so bright and cheerful and just looking at them makes me smile. I have enjoyed growing them in my garden for many years, so I suppose it was only a matter of time before I picked up a needle and started stitching them too.

You may know my work and even have one of my books in the series of *Embroidered Garden Flowers*, Sally Milner Publishing. If so, you will know that I work with a flower in front of me, matching the threads as closely as possible or blending different coloured threads in the needle to achieve the effect or colour I want. It's fun to stitch a pansy this way and see it come to life. Perhaps you might like to try it yourself.

After doing so much fine embroidery I wanted to work in a different scale. The pansies are quicker to do as well as being easier on the eyes. I embroidered my very first pansy in 1988 and the idea for this book started at that time, so it has taken 17 years for the idea to come to fruition. There have been a few detours along the way including the four other books.

I have matched all the pansies in the book to the threads and then stitched a sample of each one and written the instructions. So all the pansies were real and I have worked them in a way that I know you will be able to do too. The more experienced embroiderers and artists amongst you might just use the book as a starting off point and move on to adding more details, shading etc.

As I write this first but final chapter, I reflect on what we have come to refer to as The Pansy Journey. I shall tell you the story.

This is a very special book, not just to me but also to a group of friends who have worked with me over a long period of time on the pansies and pansy projects. They have helped me in many ways, especially over the last couple of years. Several years ago they came to a class of 'Masterpiece' pansies and I asked them afterwards if they'd like to keep meeting with me every couple of weeks. I would give them a new pansy or two to stitch and help them with their designs and projects. This commitment would keep me working on the book, as it is hard to stay focused on such a long-term project.

The members of The Pansy Group, as it became known, kept bringing me more and more beautiful pansies and of course I couldn't resist matching them with the threads. We had great fun and all became quite addicted to trying them out. I still can't resist doing this and there will always be pansies waiting for me to stitch. I hope you will enjoy them as much as we have. There is a photo of The Pansy Group at the beginning of the *Pansy Projects* chapter.

Consequently as time went by, my original idea for a book of 50 embroidered pansies became much bigger. It was hard to cut any pansies out and it really is wonderful to have so many to choose from when designing a project.

The reason it has taken so long to finish this book is because I have not been well for a long time. Finally, a diagnosis of lymphoma was made after a few years. By then I was so ill that the book seemed like an impossible dream. Working on the pansies with The Pansy Group during this difficult time had really helped me to keep going.

A very long and tough period of chemotherapy lay ahead for me and at the end of it an autologous bone marrow transplant. During my treatment and before the transplant, I managed to finish all the embroidered pansies and their instructions. So now I knew there would be a book!

Three months after the transplant I had the very good news that I was now in remission. This was six months ago. As my strength returned I threw myself back into working on the book. So now I *will* see the book!

The beautiful photos in the book were taken at a time when my garden was just brimming with pansies. Photographer Andrew Sikorski and I spent a few days working on both the photos of pansies and the projects. He finds the subject of pansies as

Diana Lampe's *Carpet of Pansies* 18.5cm (7½") x 13.5cm (5½")

delightful as I do. I am also enjoying being able to walk around my garden again.

When I first started embroidering pansies I gave them the name of the person whose garden I collected the pansy from, or the friend who brought me a lovely pansy to stitch. As time went by I decided to give all the pansies the name of a friend or family member, much nicer than just a number. This has turned out to be a most difficult task, in fact the hardest thing for me in the book! There just aren't enough pansies!

I have agonised over the names and indeed nearly removed them all a couple of times. So many people have supported me over the years, particularly the last two of my treatment. Of course I wanted to dedicate a pansy to each of them. Some friends have visited or called me every single week. What a very kind and caring thing to do for a friend and it really helped give me the strength to continue with the challenging treatment.

As one does when one's life is threatened I reviewed my life and the people who have been important to me, some from a long time ago, but not forgotten.

Sometimes a pansy is dedicated to more than one friend. This in no way means that these people are less important. There are another dozen or so people who I would have liked to include. They know who they are and they are important to me too. I will stitch some more pansies for you!

Now I will give you a little information about the book. You should be able to find your way around it easily enough by looking at the *Contents*.

Pick your Pansy will be helpful when you are choosing a pansy or looking for a particular one.

Be sure to take a little time and read through the early chapters, especially *Working Notes* and *How to Stitch a Pansy*. There is a lot of information there that has been gathered over the years and you may find something useful amongst it.

The Pansies section includes 90 pansies and the details needed to stitch them; the delightful *Heartsease* follow on.

After this you will find many beautiful *Pansy Projects* to tempt you and I'm sure you'll want to make a tea-cosy for yourself when you see Marion Tresize's *Crocheted Pansies*.

In *The Stitches* are lovely illustrations drawn by Robin Errey of all the embroidery stitches used in the book.

The *Thread Conversion Chart* shows all the threads used in the book as a reference for you. Pansies can be worked with DMC or Finca stranded cotton, Au Ver à Soie silk or Appleton's crewel wool.

The *Appendices* contain drawings of pansies, buds and leaves for you to use as well as the designs and patterns for making the projects.

I hope my experiences may inspire others to cope with some of the difficulties life dishes up. I think if you can have something else to think about and work towards it helps keep your spirits up and gives you a reason to keep going.

Even after spending so much time working with pansies, I still love them just as much as ever. Please enjoy my book; it has been a labour of love.

Diana Lampe 2005

Pick your Pansy

1 p34

2 p35

3 p36

9 p42

10 p43

11 p44

17 p50

18 p51

19 p52

25 p58

26 p59

27 p60

33 p66

34 p67

35 p68

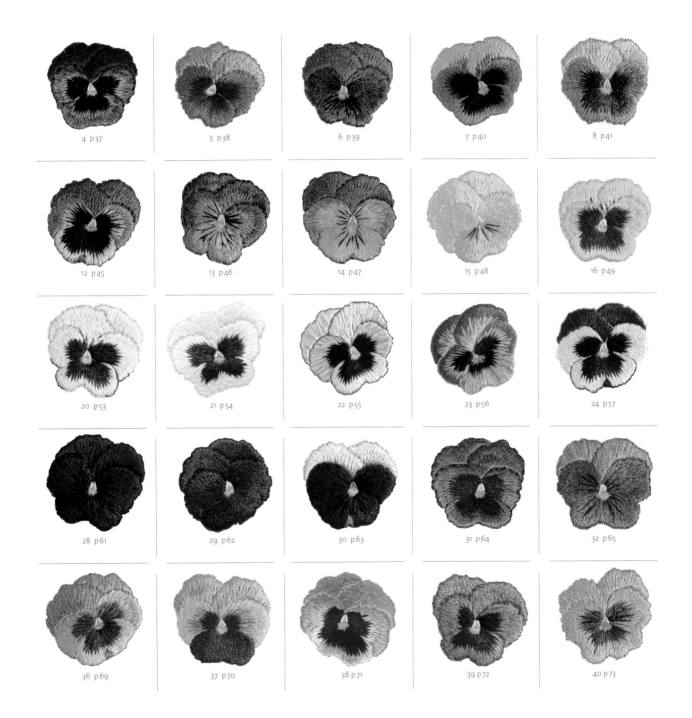

4 p37   5 p38   6 p39   7 p40   8 p41

12 p45   13 p46   14 p47   15 p48   16 p49

20 p53   21 p54   22 p55   23 p56   24 p57

28 p61   29 p62   30 p63   31 p64   32 p65

36 p69   37 p70   38 p71   39 p72   40 p73

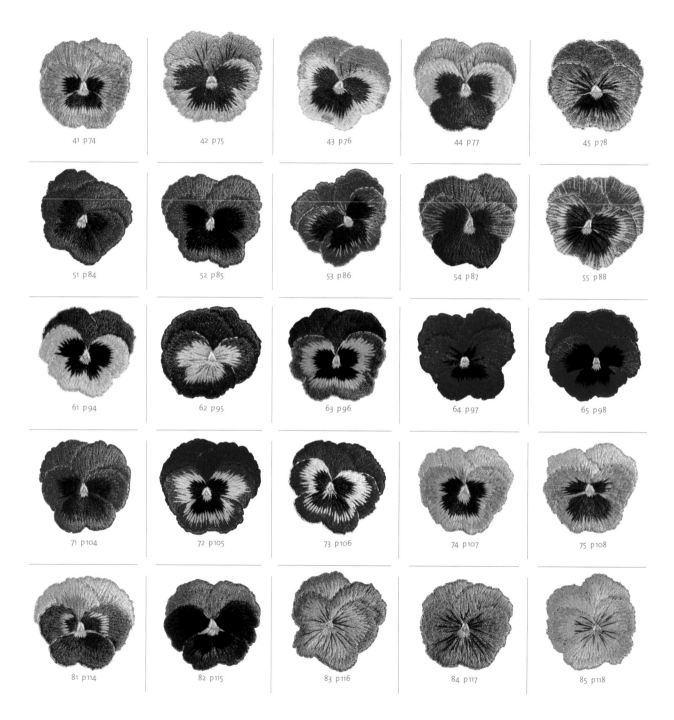

41 p74   42 p75   43 p76   44 p77   45 p78

51 p84   52 p85   53 p86   54 p87   55 p88

61 p94   62 p95   63 p96   64 p97   65 p98

71 p104   72 p105   73 p106   74 p107   75 p108

81 p114   82 p115   83 p116   84 p117   85 p118

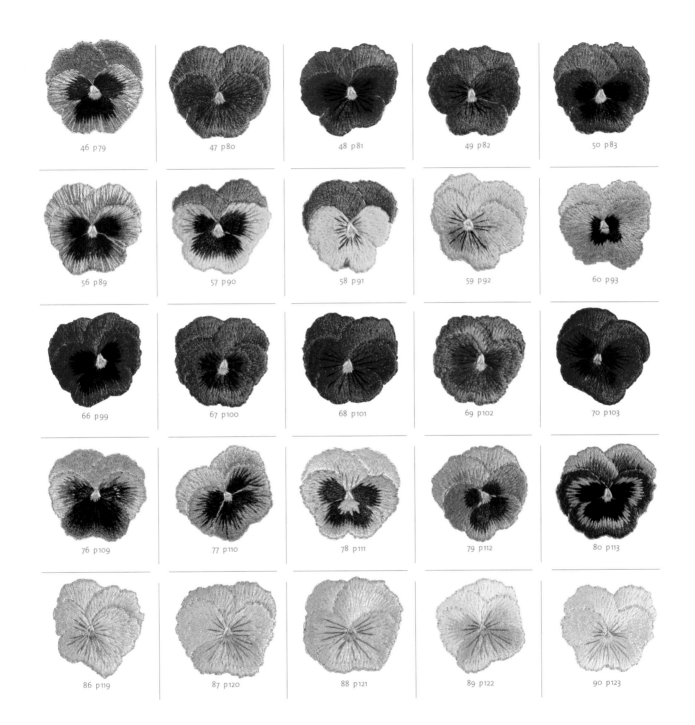

46 p79   47 p80   48 p81   49 p82   50 p83

56 p89   57 p90   58 p91   59 p92   60 p93

66 p99   67 p100   68 p101   69 p102   70 p103

76 p109   77 p110   78 p111   79 p112   80 p113

86 p119   87 p120   88 p121   89 p122   90 p123

Materials & Equipment

NEEDLES

Choose a needle with an eye that takes the thread easily. The needle should make a hole in the fabric the right size for the thread to pass through smoothly. This will prevent the thread from becoming worn.

Embroidery crewel needles are used for most surface embroidery. They have a sharp point and large eye.

Use a straw or millinery needle for bullion stitch and lazy daisy bullion stitch. The long shaft and small eye of the straw needle pass through the wraps easily, giving an even bullion stitch.

Chenille needles are generally used for crewel wool, but a large crewel needle can also be used. Chenille needles are short and sharp with a long eye and therefore easy to thread and to use.

No 7 crewel or straw needle for three strands of cotton or silk thread

No 8 crewel or straw needle for two strands of cotton or silk thread

No 9 crewel or straw needle for one strand of cotton or silk thread

No 20 or 22 chenille or No 4-5 crewel needle for crewel wool

SCISSORS

You will need a small pair of good quality embroidery scissors for cutting threads.

NEEDLE THREADERS

Use a needle threader if you have trouble threading your needle.

THIMBLES

A thimble is not really necessary but you can use one if you like.

PENCILS AND MARKERS

Water erasable fabric marking pens are the easiest thing to use for drawing pansies and designs. Be sure to remove the marks with cold water when you have finished your embroidery and before you wash it. Use a cotton wool bud dipped in water and dab it on the marks. Do not use hot water or leave your work sitting in the sun as the marks may set.

You can use a soft lead pencil (2B or HB). Make sure it is sharp and keep pencil marks light so they can easily be removed when you wash your finished embroidery. If you need to change pencil marks, rub gently with an Artgum or fabric eraser.

HOOPS

Small embroidery hoops 7.5 cm (3") or 10 cm (4") are easy to use for individual pansies and small areas of embroidery. You may like to use a bigger hoop to fit in the whole of a larger design.

Either plastic or wooden hoops are good to use. The inner ring of wooden hoops should be bound with woven cotton tape to protect your work.

THREADS

DMC stranded cotton (embroidery floss) has been used for the sample pansies and many of the designs in this book. It is a six-stranded mercerised cotton thread with a silken finish and is available in a wide range of colours. The strands can be separated and then put back together in various multiples. They can also be mixed or blended with other coloured threads for some interesting and subtle effects. Three strands have been used for the pansies in this book but smaller pansies could be worked with two strands.

Finca from Presencia is a six-stranded cotton thread (floss). It is made from the highest quality Egyptian cotton and the colours are guaranteed 100% solid dyes so they will not bleed.

Appleton's crewel wool is a two-ply twisted woollen thread. It comes in a wide range of colours and values of colours. Pansies can be worked with either one thread or two threads.

Soie d'Alger from Au Ver à Soie is a seven-stranded fine silk thread. It comes in a wide range of lovely colours and is particularly beautiful to use if you are working on a silk fabric. Silk colours are not colour fast so if your finished embroidery is soiled it will need to be dry-cleaned. Do not be tempted to wash, as the threads may bleed.

Soie d'Alger strands are a little thicker than DMC but we have still used three strands to work sample pansies. Two strands would be suitable for smaller pansies

FABRIC

Most of the projects in this book are worked on natural-coloured linen twill. This is a closely woven, strong fabric just right for stitching pansies. Linen twill is suitable to use for any of the threads suggested in this book. The right side of linen twill is the one with more obvious twill.

If you choose to work on silk, cotton or lighter weight linen, it should be backed with a lightweight cotton fabric such as homespun. Baste the two layers together and be sure to work in a hoop. The backing will add body to your fabric, making it firmer and easier to work as well as enabling you to start and finish neatly on the back.

It is important to wash and press the fabric before use, as it may shrink. If using a backing fabric this should also be washed.

Woollen fabrics such as flannel and blanketing or cashmere are suitable for working the pansies in crewel wool.

If you are uncertain about a fabric being suitable for your project, practise on a small piece first.

Working Notes for Pansies

BEFORE YOU BEGIN

Find a comfortable and well-lit place to work, gathering around everything you may need. Have some beautiful music playing in the background and the cordless phone beside you. Read carefully through the following notes before you start.

PETALS ARRANGED ON PANSY

Study a pansy closely to see the way the petals are arranged. The lower (ventral) petal sits over the side petals and to the front. The side (lateral) petals sit under the lower petal and over the upper petals. The upper (dorsal) petals are tucked in behind and overlap or underlay each other, either way. Keep this arrangement in mind as you work the pansies, particularly when stitching the outline of individual petals.

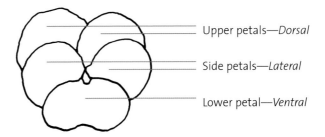

Upper petals—*Dorsal*

Side petals—*Lateral*

Lower petal—*Ventral*

1 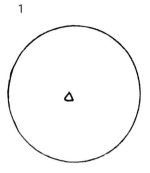 **2** 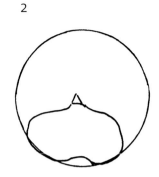 **3** 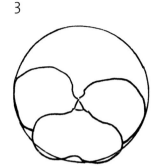 **4**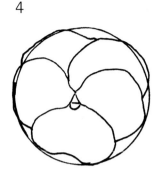

DRAWING A PANSY

This is easier to do than you may think and will enable you to draw pansies in the size you want and to work out your own designs. Study the illustrations carefully before you begin and also try to pick a fresh pansy and look at the way it is structured.

1. Draw a circle the size you want your pansy to be and add a small triangle to the centre. I used the lid of a film case for the sample pansies in this book and a large cotton reel 5 cm across for the woollen pansies.

2. Draw the lower petal first from base of triangle curving around over circle and back to triangle.

3. Add side petals from the top of triangle across and around to circle and then disappearing behind lower petal.

4. Upper petals are tucked in behind and overlap or underlay each other either way. Draw front petal first starting a little way from centre of opposite side petal, curving petal around and ending up under side petal. Draw in the other upper petal tucked in behind.

5. Draw a small semicircular shape on lower petal just below triangle for the throat of pansy.

A pansy facing to the side can be drawn easily by placing a small triangle to one side of the centre in the circle. Draw as before making petals larger on one side than the other. Pansies looking downwards or upwards can also be drawn in this way.

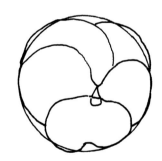

MAKING TEMPLATES

Using a template to draw around is an easy way to make your pansy look the way you want and to be the size you want. Drawings of pansies for designing and making templates can be found in the *Appendices* at the end of the book. Photocopy or trace a

pansy from the book or draw your own, then paste this onto cardboard and cut it out. Make a hole in the cardboard template for the centre and V-shaped cuts where petals curve back towards the centre.

WORKING OUT YOUR OWN DESIGNS

You may find it easier to draw your design on paper first. You can draw the design freehand or make and use templates for the pansies, leaves and buds. Build it up, pansy by pansy, overlap some, tilt them at different angles and face them in different directions. The side-view of a pansy looks effective. Finally add stems, leaves and buds until you have a well-balanced design.

BALANCE THE COLOURS

To help you achieve a balance with the colours in your design divide it roughly into three sections; this can be just in your mind. Use these sections when choosing what colour pansy to stitch. You need to consider particularly the bright, light or dark pansies, i.e. the ones that stand out the most.

Have three or more areas of a bright colour like yellow, placing at least one in each section, forming a triangle of colour. This could be just a bud or a petal. Positioning the bright colours this way will give life to your embroidery and be pleasing to the eye.

TRANSFERRING DESIGNS

Freehand or Templates

Using a water erasable marker or a sharp 2B or HB pencil draw the design freehand or with the help of templates straight onto your fabric.

Light-box

Place a copy of the design onto a light-box. You can make an improvised light-box by placing a lamp under a glass coffee table or taping the paper to a sunlit window. Position the fabric over the copy and trace the design using a water erasable pen or sharp 2B or HB pencil.

Embroidery Transfer Pencil

Trace the design onto paper. Turn the tracing over and redraw the design with a sharp embroidery transfer pencil.

It's a good idea to do a test first as some fabrics will take a transfer better than others. I find linen works very well, but silk not so well. Press a small test transfer onto either the edge of your fabric or a scrap of the same fabric.

Carefully position the tracing, transfer side down on your fabric. Press with a medium hot iron (cotton setting) for a few moments to transfer the design, taking care not to scorch the fabric. You should be able to use the transfer three times; the second time is usually the best.

USE OF THREADS

Stripping Threads

When using stranded cotton or silk it is very important to strip your threads, particularly for working long and short stitch and satin stitch. Your stitches will cover better and your work will have a smoother finish. To do this, separate the individual strands of a cut length of thread by holding it at the top and pulling one strand at a time upwards. Smooth the remaining threads before pulling out the next one. Then put back together the number of threads you need, taking care to keep them running in the same direction.

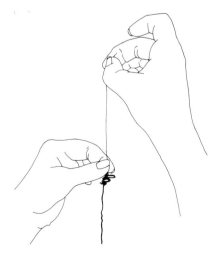

Working with the Grain

All spun thread should be worked with the grain and will unravel and wear if they are not. Thread should be used in the direction it unwinds from the skein or reel. Therefore the end you pull from a skein is the end you should thread into the needle. If you do this and take care to keep all threads running in this direction you won't have any problems.

If you are uncertain about the direction of your thread run your fingers down it to feel the grain. It will feel smooth with the grain and rough against it. Another way to tell is that the end to be threaded into a needle tends to unravel when left to rest. This fluffy end is known as the *blooming end*.

THREADING YOUR NEEDLE

Use a needle threader if you have trouble threading your needle.

Cut cotton and silk thread at a slight angle to make it easier to thread. Hold the needle steady and take the thread to it. You can also moisten the end of the thread, snipping the damp end off after threading.

To thread wool, fold the end around the needle and hold firmly with the thumb and forefinger. Remove the needle, still holding the thread firmly. Push the eye of the needle between the fingers and over the folded thread. Pull the thread through the needle. It will be easier to ask someone to show you how to do this.

USING A HOOP AND TENSION

It is important to use a hoop when stitching pansies, buds and leaves. This will help you achieve good tension and a smooth finish to your work. Adjust the fabric in the hoop making sure the grain is straight and fabric taut. Work with a stabbing motion for long and short stitch and satin stitch. Use a small hoop 7.5 cm (3") or 10 cm (4") for individual pansies. You may like to use a larger hoop to fit in the whole of a bigger design.

Take care when placing a hoop over an embroidered area. Put the edge that touches the embroidery down first. Leave stitching French knots and bullions until last.

A good tip to protect the fabric or areas already stitched is to place tissue paper over it before placing in the hoop. Tear away tissue from the area to be worked.

Don't leave your work in a hoop for very long as it may leave a mark on the fabric.

PRACTICE MAKES PERFECT

Some people find long and short stitch a little confusing at first. Before you start working a pansy, practise long and short stitch on a simple shape such as a square or rectangle. See stitch illustrations at end of book.

Don't lose heart if your first embroidered pansies are not as beautiful as you would wish. They really do take practice and after you have stitched several I'm sure you will be pleased with the result. They are great fun to do and quite addictive as well.

STARTING AND FINISHING

Avoid using knots to start your embroidery as they may show up later as a bump or shiny area.

A neat and easy way to start stitching a pansy is to use an *Away knot*. Put a knot in the end of your thread and start about 1 cm away from the pansy. Take thread through to the back and then work a couple of small backstitches on the pansy. The knot will be left on top of your work. When you have finished stitching the pansy,

turn your work over and snip off the starting threads and knots close to the edge of the pansy and remove.

Alternatively just run the starting end through the fabric under the area to be worked.

To finish off your thread, work a couple of small running stitches or backstitches under the area just worked. To keep your work neat on the back weave the tag under the embroidery and cut off the end.

Away Knot

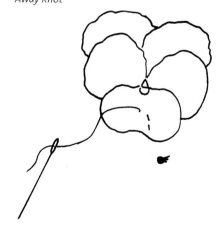

How to Stitch a Pansy

GUIDELINES

Before you start stitching a pansy draw a line with your preferred marker through the middle of each petal radiating from the centre of the pansy. This will help you with stitch direction. You can add extra lines if you wish, further dividing each petal into quarters. Please note that all lines should radiate from the pansy centre.

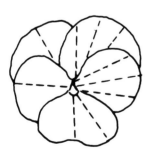

START WITH AN EASIER PANSY

I recommend you start by stitching an easier, basic pansy first. Choose one with only a couple of colours. Once you have mastered this you shouldn't have any trouble working the more detailed pansies with many different threads.

STITCHING TIPS

You will work out for yourself the most comfortable way to hold your work and the easiest and best way to stitch a pansy. Here are some tips to help you.

If you take a little care when stitching your pansy you will be rewarded with a smooth and even finish. It is important to make sure the thread isn't twisted as you work so you'll need to untwist it quite often.

I stitch away from myself and towards the edge of the pansy. You will hold the pansy upside down when working on a lower petal. Turn your work as you go so that for side petals the pansy is turned to the side and for upper petals the pansy will be the right way up.

As you pull a stitch through, place your thumb (LH) over the threads on top of your work. This will help to keep the threads flat and even. If the last stitch worked isn't sitting neatly, lift it up with your needle and then pull it down again, with thumb over threads as before.

LEAVE SPACE IN CENTRE OF PANSY

When working a pansy, take care to leave the small triangle in the centre free of stitches. Also, leave a little scallop-shaped space for the throat on lower petal just below the triangle. The throat will be added after you have stitched the petals and stripes. Throat sizes vary from pansy to pansy and so follow the instructions for a particular pansy and study the embroidered sample.

FOLLOWING THE INSTRUCTIONS

Work pansies in the order instructions

are set out, one petal at a time, i.e. lower petal first, then side petals and finally upper petals. Complete by adding stripes and outline and then throat, sides and stigma in the centre.

STITCHING THE PANSY

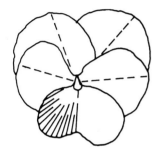

Outer Row

Outer row is the first row to be worked at the edge of a petal. Work long and short stitch from inside the petal, stitching out and down into the edge. Subsequent rows of stitching should be worked in this direction as well.

Commence stitching a petal from the middle guiding line and work one side first, then the other. Fan the stitches around the curve of the petal, working an extra short stitch or three quarter stitch if required. To achieve an even outer row on lower petal, you may need to add a couple of extra stitches at either end.

Second and Inner Rows

As you work the second and inner rows, stitch into the previous shorter stitch actually piercing the stitch. This will make the stitches merge together giving a smooth finish to your work.

Second and inner rows will have fewer stitches than the outer row. See stitching a pansy step-by-step.

You will probably need to work three rows of stitches for the lower petal on a pansy, four rows for side petals and three rows for upper petals. This will depend on the size of the pansy and the length of your stitches. Treat third and fourth rows of stitches as inner rows when following the instructions.

STRIPES

Add stripes to your pansy with long straight stitches. Follow the instructions and check the embroidered sample. Stripes are usually worked before the throat.

OUTLINE

Work around the edge of each petal with your choice of either outline stitch or backstitch. Take care to stitch the petals as they are arranged in nature. Some people choose not to work around the edges at all. Backstitch enables you to achieve a crinkly edge and it's not necessary for the stitches to be of an even length. Outline stitch gives a smoother finish.

WORKING THROAT AND CENTRE

Centres for all pansies are stitched in the same manner. You may need to adjust these instructions slightly as the space left for the centre will vary depending on how you have stitched your pansy. Be sure to check the threads used for the centre of your pansy before you start as the throats and bearded insides vary.

Throat

2 strands of 444, 972 or 742

Work the throat from pansy centre with several straight stitches radiating down into the lower petal.

Bearded Insides or Sides

2 strands 746 or listed thread, 2 bullions (No 8 straw needle) or 2 straight stitches, twice

Work the bearded insides of lateral (side) petals with a bullion stitch on either side of centre forming a triangle (5 or 6 wraps), or two straight stitches for each side, one over the other. In the instructions in this book the bearded insides of lateral petals are referred to as Sides.

Stigma

3 strands 472, French knot

Add the stigma (middle) of the pansy with a French knot (1 or 2 twists) filling the space left in the centre and tucking it firmly into place.

ADDING DETAILS TO PANSIES

As you study pansies you will notice lots of variations in their colours and markings. Some have stripes, spots or patches of colour and others have different shades even on the same petal.

Once you've mastered embroidering a pansy you may like to add some of these other details. You need to work with a pansy in front of you and be free with your stitches, adding an extra one here and there.

The colour on the edge of some pansies appears to bleed into the petal. As you work the outline add the odd little stitch, from the edge into the petal.

3 strands of chosen thread, long and short stitch

Work the bud from lower edge with long and short stitch, filling in the shape of the bud.

Outline

1 strand of thread to match bud, backstitch or stem stitch

Work around the edge of bud with either outline stitch or backstitch.

Sepals

3 strands 3347, lazy daisy bullion stitch (No 7 straw) and lazy daisy stitch or stem stitch and lazy daisy stitch

Working from the top of the bud stitch three sepals each with a lazy daisy bullion stitch (4 wraps). Work a sepal on either side of the bud and one over the bud. As you stitch each sepal curve the lazy daisy bullion to one side. To complete sepals add three or four small lazy daisy stitches above bud. Don't finish off the thread just yet, as you will need to use it for working the stem.

Sepals can be worked with stem stitch for a more realistic effect. Work sepals with two rows of stem stitch lying side by side and add a stitch at the end forming a point. Add three or four lazy daisy stitches above bud.

STEMS

3 strands 3347, stem stitch

Add the stem to your bud or pansy with stem stitch.

LEAVES

3 strands 3346 or blend 937 with 3362, slanted satin stitch

Draw a leaf with a scalloped edge where required and mark the central vein. Start stitching at the base of leaf and work with a slanted satin stitch along one side and back down the other side. To help keep your stitches slanting at the right angle, draw some guiding lines with a pencil or marker. If your satin stitches are still becoming too straight, work a half-stitch to correct the angle.

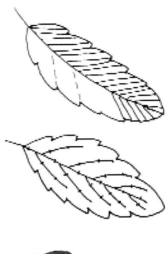

Stalk

If you wish to add a stalk to a leaf, just work a straight stitch using either the thread used for the leaf or a stem

Veins

1 strand 471 or 3347, couching

For veins, choose a lighter thread than the one you have used for the leaf. Work a long central vein with several branching veins in couching.

Outline

1 strand 3346 or 937, backstitch

Work outline of leaf with backstitch using the same thread as for the leaf.

THREAD CONVERSION CHART FOR STEMS AND LEAVES				
Threads	Leaves and outline		Leaf veins	Stems
DMC	3346	937/3362	471, 3347	3347
Finca	4561	4823	4885	4885
Appleton's	545, 546	356	543, 354, 544, 355	544, 355
Soie d'Alger	2115	2126	2114, 2124, 2125	2114, 2125

Note: Anchor stranded cotton 268 is a perfect match for pansy leaves and has been used for some designs in this book.

PANSIES IN WOOL

Working pansies in wool is not very different to working them with stranded cotton. Everything is just a little bigger. Study the step-by-step pansy in wool before you begin. As the pansy is larger and threads are thicker your stitches will need to be correspondingly longer and placed a little more sparsely. You will find your pansies bloom quickly when worked in wool.

The woollen pansies featured in the projects in this book are quite large. I would stitch them with two threads and the details with one. Dianne Smith's beautiful blanket, see *Pansy Projects* chapter, was worked with one thread throughout. So if you want to take more time and achieve a finer finish, use just one thread. Smaller woollen pansies could be worked with one thread.

A good size pansy to stitch with two threads of Appleton's is about 5 cm (2 ½") across. See drawings of pansies for wool in the *Appendices* or refer to DRAWING A PANSY and MAKING TEMPLATES in the chapter *Working Notes for Pansies*.

I suggest you substitute two threads of Appleton's crewel wool where three strands of DMC stranded cotton are listed and one thread of wool when one strand of cotton is listed.

Where threads are blended the effect will be slightly different when you use one thread of each colour in wool, so if this bothers you, stitch the two colours separately. Work the main colour first, stitching quite closely and then stitch the other colour sparsely over the first.

Remember to place your work in a hoop.

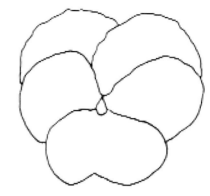

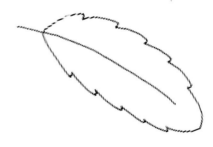

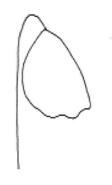

Step-by-step pansies in wool

Finishing & Framing

FINISHING OFF

When you have finished embroidering your project, be sure to sign and date it. Do this in stem stitch or backstitch using one strand of a soft green or a thread used in the design.

Tidy up the back of your work making sure there are no untidy tags left and beginnings and endings are secure. Stray tags could show through when your embroidery is framed.

WASHING AND PRESSING

Washing your finished embroidery will really bring it to life. These instructions are for DMC, Finca and Appleton's threads. Au Ver à Soie should not be washed as the colours may bleed.
If you have used silk and your finished embroidery is soiled it will have to be dry-cleaned.

Hand wash your finished piece in cold or lukewarm water using soft soap. Don't soak as some deeply shaded threads may bleed. Rinse well, but don't wring, instead roll in a towel to remove excess moisture. Don't leave your embroidery sitting around wet, press it straight away.

Place embroidery face down on a towel overlaid with a pressing cloth. Place another cloth over the embroidery and press with a fairly hot iron until nearly dry. Remove the cloth and finish pressing the embroidery, taking care not to scorch it.

FRAMING

Your finished embroidery should be laced before framing. Some framers will do this for you or you can do it yourself.

Take your finished embroidery to a good framer who knows how to conserve and frame needlework. The mount and frame should complement the embroidered design and the framer will help you make a choice.

CARE OF YOUR EMBROIDERY

Take care of your embroidery and don't leave it near a window as the light will fade it.

The Pansies

In this section are instructions and details for 90 different pansies, 14 of them having a variation.

The instructions for each pansy include, a list of the threads used, picture of a sample pansy, all details needed to work the pansy and a thread conversion chart.

Pansies are arranged by colour, in a way designed for you to find easy to use. Refer to *Pick your Pansy* at the front of the book to help you quickly find a particular pansy.

Pansies can be worked in different sizes using the different threads listed. All sample pansies are worked with DMC stranded cotton and thread numbers appear with the instructions. If you wish to use Finca, Soie d'Alger or Appleton's refer to the individual conversion chart and then replace thread numbers with your choice.

SIZES AND MEDIUMS

You may like to experiment with different size pansies, different mediums and the number of strands used. Drawings of pansies in different sizes can be found in the *Appendices*. Some suggestions for you to try are:

DMC or Finca stranded cotton
3 strands for sample size pansy or 2 strands for smaller pansies

Soie d'Alger
3 strands for sample size pansy or 2 strands for smaller pansies

Appleton's crewel wool
1 or 2 threads for large pansy or 1 thread for smaller (sample size) pansy

Before you start work on a pansy read through *Working Notes for Pansies* and *How to Stitch a Pansy*.

1. Violet and Navy Pansy

THREADS

DMC 333, 939, (444, 472, 746)
Work petals for pansy with long and short stitch leaving the centre triangle and space for throat free of stitches.

LOWER PETAL

Outer row—3 strands 333
Second and inner rows—3 strands 939

SIDE PETALS

Outer and second row—3 strands 333
Inner rows—3 strands 939

UPPER PETALS

All rows—3 strands 333

STRIPES

Upper petals—1 strand 939, straight stitch
Add 2 or 3 stripes to inner row of upper petals

OUTLINE

All petals—1 strand 333, backstitch or outline stitch

CENTRE

Throat—2 strands 444, straight stitches
Sides—2 strands 746, straight stitches or bullion stitches
Stigma—3 strands 472, French knot

THREADS	PETALS		THROAT & CENTRE		
DMC	333	939	444	472	746
Finca	2699*	3327	1227	4799	1211
Appleton's	895	852	553	251A	871
Au ver a soie	1344	163	536	2123	crème

For Rosanna Hindmarsh

2. Striped Violet & Blue with Navy Pansy

THREADS

DMC 333, 791, 939, (444, 472, 746)
Work petals for pansy with long and short stitch leaving the centre triangle and space for throat free of stitches.

LOWER PETAL

Outer row–blend 2 strands 333 and 1 strand of 791

Inner rows–blend 2 strands 939 and 1 strand 791

SIDE PETALS

Outer row–blend 2 strands 333 and 1 strand 791

Inner rows–blend 2 strands 939 and 1 strand 791

UPPER PETALS

All rows–blend 2 strands 333 and 1 strand 791

STRIPES

Upper petals–1 strand 939, straight stitches

Add a few stripes to upper petals

OUTLINE

All petals–1 strand 939, backstitch or outline stitch

CENTRE

Throat–2 strands 444, straight stitches

Sides–2 strands 746, straight stitches or bullion stitches

Stigma–3 strands 472, French knot

THREADS	PETALS			THROAT & CENTRE		
DMC	333	791	939	444	472	746
Finca	2699*	3324*	3327	1227	4799	1211
Appleton's	895	896	852	553	251A	871
Soie d'Alger	1344	4916	163	536	2123	crème

For Tiina Johnston

3. Violet & Purple Pansy

THREADS
DMC 333, 550, 939, (444, 472, 746)
Work petals for pansy with long and short stitch leaving the centre triangle and space for throat free of stitches.

LOWER PETAL
Outer and second rows–3 strands 333
Inner row–3 strands 550

SIDE PETALS
Outer and second rows–3 strands 333
Inner row–3 strands 550

UPPER PETALS
All rows–3 strands 333

STRIPES
Side and lower petals–1 strand 939, straight stitches
Upper petals–1 strand 550, straight stitches

Add several long navy blue stripes to lower petal, about four to side petals and a few purple ones to upper petals

OUTLINE
All petals–1 strand 550, backstitch or outline stitch

CENTRE
Throat–2 strands 444, straight stitches
Sides–2 strands 746, straight stitches or bullion stitches
Stigma–3 strands 472, French knot

Variation: for a different version of this pansy work upper petals with 550 and don't add the stripes

THREADS	PETALS			THROAT & CENTRE		
DMC	333	550	939	444	472	746
Finca	2699*	2635*	3327	1227	4799	1211
Appleton's	895	456	852	553	251A	871
Soie d'Alger	1344	3316	163	536	2123	crème

For Jenny and Whitney Brennan

4. Violet, Purple & Navy Pansy

THREADS

DMC 333, 550, 791, 939, 3746, (444, 472, 746)

Work petals for pansy with long and short stitch leaving the centre triangle and space for throat free of stitches.

LOWER PETAL

Outer row–blend 2 strands 333 and 1 strand 791

Second row–3 strands 3746

Inner row–3 strands 550

SIDE PETALS

Outer row–blend 2 strands 333 and 1 strand 791

Second row–3 strands 3746

Inner row–3 strands 550

UPPER PETALS

All rows–3 strands 550

STRIPES

Lower and side petals–1 strand 939, straight stitches

Add several stripes to lower petal and about four to side petals

OUTLINE

All petals–1 strand 550, backstitch or outline stitch

CENTRE

Throat–2 strands 444, straight stitches

Sides–2 strands 746, straight stitches or bullion stitches

Stigma–3 strands 472, French knot

Variation: for a slightly different version of this pansy work inner rows with 939 instead of 550 and don't add the stripes

THREADS	PETALS					THROAT & CENTRE		
DMC	333	550	791	939	3746	444	472	746
Finca	2699*	2635*	3324*	3327	2699	1227	4799	1211
Appleton's	895	456	896	852	894	553	251A	871
Soie d'Alger	1344	3316	4916	163	1343	536	2123	crème

For Joanie Lampe

5. Blue & Brown Pansy

THREADS

DMC 340, 341, 550, 801, 938, 3740, 3746, (444, 472, 746)

Work petals for pansy with long and short stitch leaving the centre triangle and space for throat free of stitches.

LOWER PETAL

Outer row–3 strands 3746

Second row–3 strands 801

Inner rows–2 strands 550 and 1 strand 938

SIDE PETALS

Outer row–3 strands 3746 (or 2 strands 3746 and 1 strand 340)

Second row–3 strands 3740

Inner rows–3 strands 550

UPPER PETALS

All rows–blend 2 strands 340 and 1 strand 341

Stripes–1 strand 3740, straight stitches

Add a few stripes to upper petals

OUTLINE

All petals–1 strand 340, backstitch or outline stitch

CENTRE

Throat–2 strands 444, straight stitches

Sides–2 strands 746, straight stitches or bullion stitches

Stigma–3 strands 472, French knot

THREADS	PETALS							THROAT & CENTRE		
DMC	340	341	550	801	938	3740	3746	444	472	746
Finca	2699*	2732	2635*	8080	8171	8620*	2699	1227	4799	1211
Appleton's	893	892	456	304	582	605	894	553	251A	871
Soie d'Alger	1343	4912	3316	4116	4132	4635*	1343	536	2123	crème

For David and Georgina Lampe

6. Cornflower Blue Pansy

THREADS

DMC 333, 823, 3746, (444, 472, 746)
Work petals for pansy with long and
short stitch leaving the centre triangle
and space for throat free of stitches.

LOWER PETAL

All rows–blend 2 strands 3746
and 1 strand 333

SIDE PETALS

All rows–blend 2 strands 3746
and 1 strand 333

UPPER PETALS

All rows–3 strands 3746

OUTLINE

All petals–1 strand 3746, backstitch
or outline stitch

STRIPES

Lower and side petals–1 strand 823,
straight stitches

Add lots of long stripes to lower petal
and several shorter ones to side petals

CENTRE

Throat–2 strands 444, straight stitches

Work quite a big throat well down
into the lower petal

Sides–2 strands 746, straight stitches
or bullion stitches

Stigma–3 strands 472, French knot

THREADS	PETALS			THROAT & CENTRE		
DMC	333	823	3746	444	472	746
Finca	2699*	3327*	2699	1227	4799	1211
Appleton's	895	106	894	553	251A	871
Soie d'Alger	1344	161	1343	536	2123	crème

For David Forman and Sara York

7. Shades of Blue & Navy Pansy

THREADS

DMC 211, 340, 550, 791, 3746, 3747, (444, 472, 746)

Work petals for pansy with long and short stitch leaving the centre triangle and space for throat free of stitches.

LOWER PETAL

Outer row–3 strands 340

Inner rows–3 strands 791

SIDE PETALS

Outer row–3 strands 340

Second row–3 strands 3746

Inner row–3 strands 791

UPPER PETALS

Outer and second rows–blend 2 strands 3747 and 1 strand 211

Inner row–3 strands 3746

Work a few stitches for final row to add a deeper shade to base of petals

STRIPES

Side and lower petals–1 strand 550, straight stitches

Add several long stripes to lower petal and about five slightly shorter ones to side petals

OUTLINE

Lower and side petals–1 strand 340, backstitch or outline stitch

Upper petals–1 strand 3747

CENTRE

Throat–2 strands 444, straight stitches

Sides–2 strands 746, straight stitches or bullion stitches

Stigma–3 strands 472, French knot

Variation: inner rows could be worked with 333 or with a blend of 333 and 791

THREADS	PETALS						THROAT & CENTRE		
DMC	211	340	550	791	3746	3747	444	472	746
Finca	2687	2699*	2635*	3324*	2699	2729	1227	4799	1211
Appleton's	884	893	456	896	894	886	553	251A	871
Soie d'Alger	3322*	1343	3316	4916	1343	4911	536	2123	crème

For Carolyn Banbury

8. Shades of Light Blue & Violet Pansy

THREADS

DMC 210, 211, 333, 340, 3747, (444, 472, 746)

Work petals for pansy with long and short stitch leaving the centre triangle and space for throat free of stitches.

LOWER PETAL

Outer row–3 strands 340

Inner rows–3 strands 333

SIDE PETALS

Outer rows–blend 2 strands 340 and 1 strand 210

Second rows–3 strands 340

Inner rows–3 strands 333

UPPER PETALS

All rows–blend 2 strands 3747 and 1 strand 211

OUTLINE

All petals–1 strand 3747, backstitch or outline stitch

CENTRE

Throat–2 strands 444, straight stitches

Sides–2 strands 746, straight stitches or bullion stitches

Stigma–3 strands 472, French knot

THREADS	PETALS					THROAT & CENTRE		
DMC	210	211	333	340	3747	444	472	746
Finca	2606	2687	2699*	2699*	2729	1227	4799	1211
Appleton's	885	884	895	893	886	553	251A	871
Soie d'Alger	3334*	3322*	1344	1343	4911	536	2123	crème

For Jan Jolliffe

9. Shades of Light Blue, White & Violet Pansy

THREADS

DMC 211, 333, 340, 746, 3747,
(444, 472, 746)

Work petals for pansy with long
and short stitch leaving the centre
triangle and space for throat free
of stitches.

LOWER PETAL

Outer row–3 strands 340

Second row–3 strands 746

Inner rows–3 strands 333

SIDE PETALS

Outer row–blend 2 strands 3747
and 1 strand 211

Second row–3 strands 340

Third row–2 strands 746

Inner rows–3 strands 333

UPPER PETALS

Outer and second rows–blend 2
strands 3747 and 1 strand 211

Inner row–3 strands 340

Work a few stitches for inner row to
add a deeper shade to base of petals

OUTLINE

All petals–1 strand 3747, backstitch or
outline stitch

CENTRE

Throat–2 strands 444, straight stitches

Sides–2 strands 746, straight stitches
or bullion stitches

Stigma–3 strands 472, French knot

THREADS	PETALS				THROAT & CENTRE		
DMC	211	333	340	3747	444	472	746
Finca	2687	2699*	2699*	2729	1227	4799	1211
Appleton's	884	895	893	886	553	251A	871
Soie d'Alger	3322*	1344	1343	4911	536	2123	crème

For Jo Pie
For Sarah Strasser

10. Cornflower Blue, White & Navy Pansy

THREADS

DMC 333, 340, 746, 791, 939, 3746, (444, 472, 746)

Work petals for pansy with long and short stitch leaving the centre triangle and space for throat free of stitches.

LOWER PETAL

Outer row–3 strands 3746

Second row–3 strands 746

Inner rows–3 strands 791

SIDE PETALS

Outer row–3 strands 3746

Second row–3 strands 333

Third row and fourth row–3 strands 746

Inner row–3 strands 791

Inner row for this pansy is quite small so needs only a few stitches

UPPER PETALS

Outer and second rows–3 strands 340

Inner row–3 strands 333

Work a few stitches for final row to add a touch of purple to base of petals

STRIPES

Side and lower petals–1 strand 939, straight stitches

Add several long stripes to lower petal and about four or five shorter ones to side petals

OUTLINE

Lower and side petals–1 strand 746, backstitch or outline stitch

Upper petals–1 strand 340, backstitch or outline stitch

CENTRE

Throat–2 strands 444, straight stitches

Sides–2 strands 746, straight stitches or bullion stitches

Stigma–3 strands 472, French knot

THREADS	PETALS					THROAT & CENTRE		
DMC	333	340	791	939	3746	444	472	746
Finca	2699*	2699*	3324*	3327	2699	1227	4799	1211
Appleton's	895	893	896	852	894	553	251A	871
Soie d'Alger	1344	1343	4916	163	1343	536	2123	crème

For Carolyn Pennington

11. Pale Mauve, Blue & Purple Pansy

THREADS

DMC 210, 211, 333, 340, 550, 938, 3743, (444, 472, 746)

Work petals for pansy with long and short stitch leaving the centre triangle and space for throat free of stitches.

LOWER PETAL

Outer row–blend 2 strands 340 and 1 strand 210

Inner rows–2 strands 550 and 1 strand 938

SIDE PETALS

Outer and second rows–blend 2 strands 340 and 1 strand 210

Inner rows–3 strands 333

UPPER PETALS

All rows–blend 2 strands 211 and 1 strand 3743

STRIPES

Side petals–1 strand 550, straight stitches

Add about five stripes to side petals

OUTLINE

Side and lower petals–1 strand 340, backstitch or outline stitch

Upper petals–1 strand 211, backstitch or outline stitch

CENTRE

Throat–2 strands 444, straight stitches

Work quite a big throat well down into the lower petal

Sides–2 strands 746, straight stitches or bullion stitches

Stigma–3 strands 472, French knot

THREADS	PETALS							THROAT & CENTRE		
DMC	210	211	333	340	550	938	3743	444	472	746
Finca	2606	2687	2699*	2699*	2635*	8171	8599	1227	4799	1211
Appleton's	885	884	895	893	456	582	891	553	251A	871
Soie d'Alger	3334*	3322*	1344	1343	3316	4132	3332	536	2123	crème

For Norelle Williams

12. Blue, Lemon & Maroon Pansy

THREADS

DMC 154, 155, 208, 445, 550, 3078, 3746, (444, 472, 746)

Work petals for pansy with long and short stitch leaving the centre triangle and space for throat free of stitches.

LOWER PETAL

Outer row–3 strands 445

Inner rows–3 strands 154

SIDE PETALS

Outer row–3 strands 155

Second and third row–blend 2 strands 3078 and 1 strand 155

Inner row–3 strands 550

UPPER PETALS

Outer row–blend 2 strands 3746 and 1 strand 208

Inner rows–3 strands 3746

MARKINGS

'V' mark–3 strands 3746, straight stitches

Add a 'V' shaped mark to edge of lower petal, halfway around with four small stitches. See embroidered sample

Stripes to edge–1 strand 3746

Add a few very small straight stitches to edge of petal on either side of 'V'

STRIPES

Side and lower petals–1 strand 550, straight stitches

Add several long stripes to lower petal and four or five shorter stripes to side petals

OUTLINE

All petals–1 strand 208, backstitch or outline stitch

CENTRE

Throat–2 strands 972, straight stitches

Sides–2 strands 746, straight stitches or bullion stitches

Stigma–3 strands 472, French knot

THREADS	PETALS							THROAT & CENTRE		
DMC	154	155	208	445	550	3078	3746	444	472	746
Finca	—	2699	2615	1217	2635*	1214	2699	1227	4799	1211
Appleton's	607	894	454	551	456	841	894	553	251A	871
Soie d'Alger	5116	1343	1334	2523	3316	2121	1343	536	2123	crème

For Margot Fenner

13. Cornflower Blue & Yellow Pansy

THREADS

DMC 307, 333, 340, 341, 444, 791, 3746, (472, 746, 972)

Work petals for pansy with long and short stitch leaving the centre triangle and space for throat free of stitches.

LOWER PETAL

Outer row–3 strands 340

Second row–3 strands 307

Inner row–3 strands 444

SIDE PETALS

Outer row–3 strands 3746

Second row–3 strands 340

Inner row–blend 2 strands 341 and 1 strand 340

UPPER PETALS

Outer row–3 strands 333

Inner rows–3 strands 3746

STRIPES

Side and lower petals–1 strand 791, straight stitches

Add several long branching, long stripes to lower petal. Add four or five shorter stripes to side petals. Stripes on side petals are heavier than usual so work two stitches for each, one over the other.

OUTLINE

All petals–1 strand 333, backstitch or outline stitch

CENTRE

Throat–2 strands 972, straight stitches

Work a good sized, rounded throat down into the lower petal

Sides–2 strands 746, straight stitches or bullion stitches

Stigma–3 strands 472, French knot

THREADS	PETALS							THROAT & CENTRE		
DMC	307	333	340	341	444	791	3746	472	746	972
Finca	1222	2699*	2699*	2732	1227	3324*	2699	4799	1211	1232
Appleton's	552*	895	893	892	553	896	894	251A	871	555
Soie d'Alger	535*	1344	1343	4912	536	4916	1343	2123	crème	545

For Judy Hincksman
For Katrin von Ribbeck

14. Yellow, Cornflower & Lemon Pansy

THREADS

MC 307, 333, 340, 444, 445, 939, 3746, (472, 746, 972)

Work petals for pansy with long and short stitch leaving the centre triangle and space for throat free of stitches.

LOWER PETAL

All rows–3 strands 444

SIDE PETALS

Outer row–blend 2 strands 340 and 1 strand 307

Inner rows–blend 2 strands 307 and 1 strand 445

UPPER PETALS

All rows–3 strands 3746

STRIPES

Side and lower petals–1 strand 939, straight stitches

Add several medium length stripes to lower petal and four or five shorter ones to side petals.

MARKINGS

Lower petal–1 strand 3746, straight stitches

Work a 'V' shaped mark halfway around petal with short stitches. Add stitches to edge of petal on either side of 'V' as well. See embroidered sample

OUTLINE

All petals–1 strand 333, backstitch or outline stitch

CENTRE

Throat–2 strands 972, straight stitches

Work a good sized and rounded throat down into the lower petal

Sides–2 strands 746, straight stitches or bullion stitches

Stigma–3 strands 472, French knot

THREADS	PETALS							THROAT & CENTRE		
DMC	307	333	340	444	445	939	3746	472	746	972
Finca	1222	2699*	2699*	1227	1217	3327	2699	4799	1211	1232
Appleton's	552*	895	893	553	551	852	894	251A	871	555
Soie d'Alger	535*	1344	1343	536	2523	163	1343	2123	crème	545

For Katina Barrack
For Deborah Webb

15. Yellow & Bright Lemon Pansy

THREADS

DMC 307, 444, 3371, (444, 472, 746)
Work petals for pansy with long
and short stitch leaving the centre
triangle and space for throat free
of stitches.

LOWER PETAL

All rows–3 strands 444

SIDE PETALS

All rows–3 strands 307

UPPER PETALS

All rows–3 strands 307

STRIPES

Lower petal–1 strand 3371,
straight stitches
Add six fine stripes to the lower petal

OUTLINE

All petals–1 strand 307, backstitch
or outline stitch

CENTRE

Throat–2 strands 444, straight stitches
Sides–2 strands 746, straight stitches
or bullion stitches
Stigma–3 strands 472, French knot

THREADS	PETALS		THROAT & CENTRE		
DMC	307	3371	444	472	746
Finca	1222	8083	1227	4799	1211
Appleton's	552*	587	553	251A	871
Soie d'Alger	535*	4146	536	2123	crème

For Anne Coupland

16. Yellow & Tan Pansy

THREADS

DMC 300, 444, (444, 472, 746)
Work petals for pansy with long
and short stitch leaving the centre
triangle and space for throat free
of stitches.

LOWER PETALS

Outer row–3 strands 444

Second and inner rows–3 strands 300

SIDE PETALS

Outer and second row–3 strands 444

Inner rows–3 strands 300

UPPER PETALS

All rows–3 strands 444

Stripes–2 strands 300,
straight stitches

Add a few stripes to upper petals

OUTLINE

All petals–1 strand 444, backstitch
or outline stitch

CENTRE

Throat–2 strands 444, straight stitches

Sides–2 strands 746, straight stitches
or bullion stitches

Stigma–3 strands 472, French knot

THREADS	PETALS	THROAT & CENTRE		
DMC	300	444	472	746
Finca	7656*	1227	4799	1211
Appleton's	767	553	251A	871
Soie d'Alger	4215	536	2123	crème

For Sue Gage

17. Yellow & Dark Brown Pansy

THREADS

DMC 444, 938, 3371 (472, 746, 972)

Work petals for pansy with long and short stitch leaving the centre triangle and space for throat free of stitches.

LOWER PETAL

Outer row–3 strands 444

Inner rows–blend 2 strands 938 and 1 strand 3371 (or 3 strands 938)

SIDE PETALS

Outer and second rows–3 strands 444

Inner row–3 strands 938

UPPER PETALS

All rows–3 strands 444

Stripes–2 strands 938, straight stitches

Add two or three stripes to inner row if desired

OUTLINE

All petals–1 strand 444, backstitch or outline stitch

CENTRE

Throat–2 strands 972, straight stitches

Sides–2 strands 746, straight stitches or bullion stitches

Stigma–3 strands 472, French knot

THREADS	PETALS			THROAT & CENTRE		
DMC	444	938	3371	472	746	972
Finca	1227	8171	8083	4799	1211	1232
Appleton's	553	582	587	251A	871	555
Soie d'Alger	536	4132	4146	2123	crème	545

For Judy Brien
For Chris Harris

18. Yellow, Purple & Black Brown Pansy

THREADS
DMC 444, 550, 3371, (444, 472, 746)
Work petals for pansy with long and short stitch leaving the centre triangle and space for throat free of stitches.

LOWER PETAL
Outer and second rows–3 strands 444
Inner row–3 strands 3371

SIDE PETALS
Outer, second and third rows–3 strands 444
Inner row–3 strands 3371

UPPER PETALS
All rows–3 strands 550

OUTLINE
Lower and side petals–1 strand 444, backstitch or outline stitch
Upper petals–1 strand 550, backstitch or outline stitch

CENTRE
Throat–2 strands 444, straight stitches
Sides–2 strands 746, straight stitches or bullion stitches
Stigma–3 strands 472, French knot

Variation: Add a few stitches with 3 strands 550 for patches of purple to lower and side petals. See yellow, pink and maroon pansy No 43

THREADS	PETALS		THROAT & CENTRE		
DMC	550	3371	444	472	746
Finca	2635*	8083	1227	4799	1211
Appleton's	456	587	553	251A	871
Soie d'Alger	3316	4146	536	2123	crème

For Sue Spork

19. Lemon, Purple & Maroon Pansy

THREADS

DMC 307, 550, 727, 902, 3740, (472, 746, 972)

Work petals for pansy with long and short stitch leaving the centre triangle and space for throat free of stitches.

LOWER PETAL

Outer row–3 strands 307

Inner rows–3 strands 902 (or 2 strands 902 and 1 strand 550)

SIDE PETALS

Outer row–3 strands 727

Inner rows–2 strands 550 and 1 strand 902

UPPER PETALS

All rows–3 strands 727

Stripes–1 strand each 550 and 902, straight stitches

Add a few stripes to inner row

OUTLINE

All petals–1 strand 3740 (or 727), backstitch or outline stitch

CENTRE

Throat–2 strands 972, straight stitches

Sides–2 strands 746, straight stitches or bullion stitches

Stigma–3 strands 472, French knot

Note: Underside of petals or a bud could be worked with 3041

THREADS	PETALS					THROAT & CENTRE		
DMC	307	550	727	902	3740	472	746	972
Finca	1222	2635*	1134*	2171	8620*	4799	1211	1232
Appleton's	552*	456	996	149	605	251A	871	555
Soie d'Alger	535*	3316	521	4625	4635*	2123	crème	545

For Del Gordon

20. Lemon & Purple Pansy

THREADS

DMC 445, 550, 902, 3078, 3743, (444, 472, 746)

Work petals for pansy with long and short stitch leaving the centre triangle and space for throat free of stitches.

LOWER PETAL

Outer row–3 strands 445

Inner rows–blend 2 strands 550 and 1 strand 902

SIDE PETALS

Outer rows–blend 2 strands 3078 and 1 strand 445

Inner rows–3 strands 550

UPPER PETALS

All rows–blend 2 strands 3078 and 1 strand 3743

Stripes–1 strand 550, straight stitches

Add a few stripes to inner row if desired

OUTLINE

All petals–1 strand 445 with touches of 550 (see sample), backstitch or outline stitch

CENTRE

Throat–2 strands 444, straight stitches

Sides–2 strands 746, straight stitches or bullion stitches

Stigma–3 strands 472, French knot

THREADS	PETALS					THROAT & CENTRE		
DMC	445	550	902	3078	3743	444	472	746
Finca	1217	2635*	2171	1214	8599	1227	4799	1211
Appleton's	551	456	149	841	891	553	251A	871
Soie d'Alger	2523	3316	4625	2121	3332	536	2123	crème

For Sue Gardner
For Cleo Parsons

21. Cream & Purple Pansy

THREADS

DMC 550, 902, 3823, (444, 472, 746)

Work petals for pansy with long and short stitch leaving the centre triangle and space for throat free of stitches.

LOWER PETAL

Outer and second row–3 strands 3823

Inner rows–2 strands 550 and 1 strand 902 (or 3 strands 550)

SIDE PETALS

Outer and second rows–3 strands 3823

Inner rows–3 strands 550

UPPER PETALS

All rows–3 strands 3823

OUTLINE

All petals–1 strand 3823, backstitch or outline stitch

CENTRE

Throat–2 strands 444, straight stitches

Sides–2 strands 746, straight stitches or bullion stitches

Stigma–3 strands 472, French knot

THREADS	PETALS			THROAT & CENTRE		
DMC	550	902	3823	444	472	746
Finca	2635*	2171	1128	1227	4799	1211
Appleton's	456	149	872	553	251A	871
Soie d'Alger	3316	4625	531	536	2123	crème

For Sarah Firth

22. Striped Cream & Lavender with Purple Pansy

THREADS

DMC 745, 550, 3042, 3740, (444, 472, 746)
Work petals for pansy with long and short stitch leaving the centre triangle and space for throat free of stitches.

LOWER PETAL

Outer row–3 strands 745
Inner rows–3 strands 550

SIDE PETALS

Outer and second rows–blend 2 strands 745 and 1 strand 3042
Inner rows–3 strands 550

UPPER PETALS

All rows–blend 2 strands 745 and 1 strand 3042

STRIPES

Upper petals–1 strand 3740, straight stitches

Add 2 or 3 stripes over inner row of upper petals. Work at the same time as outline.

OUTLINE

All petals–1 strand 3740, backstitch or outline stitch

CENTRE

Throat–2 strands 444, straight stitches
Sides–2 strands 746, straight stitches or bullion stitches
Stigma–3 strands 472, French knot

THREADS	PETALS				THROAT & CENTRE		
DMC	745	550	3042	3740	444	472	746
Finca	1137	2635*	8605	8620*	1227	4799	1211
Appleton's	471	456	603	605	553	251A	871
Soie d'Alger	2531	3316	5112	4635*	536	2123	crème

For Halska Markowski
For Diana Harberecht

23. Lavender, Cream & Purple Pansy

THREADS

DMC 444, 550, 938, 3041, 3078,
(444, 472, 746)

Work petals for pansy with long and short stitch leaving the centre triangle and space for throat free of stitches.

LOWER PETAL

Outer row–blend 2 strands 3078 and 1 strand 3041

Second row–3 strands 444

Inner rows–3 strands 938

SIDE PETALS

Outer row–3 strands 3041

Second row–3 strands 3078

Inner rows–3 strands 550

UPPER PETALS

Outer row–3 strands 3041

Second and inner rows–3 strands 3078

OUTLINE

Upper petals–1 strand 3041, backstitch or outline stitch

Side and lower petals–1 strand 3078, backstitch or outline stitch

CENTRE

Throat–2 strands 444, straight stitches

This pansy has quite a pronounced throat so make the stitches a little longer than usual

Sides–2 strands 746, straight stitches or bullion stitches

Stigma–3 strands 472, French knot

THREADS	PETALS				THROAT & CENTRE		
DMC	550	938	3041	3078	444	472	746
Finca	2635*	8171	8620	1214	1227	4799	1211
Appleton's	456	582	933	841	553	251A	871
Soie d'Alger	3316	4132	5113	2121	536	2123	crème

For Maggie Taylor

24. Cream, Maroon & Purple Pansy

THREADS
DMC 550, 746, 902, 3078, (444, 472, 746)
Work petals for pansy with long and short stitch leaving the centre triangle and space for throat free of stitches.

LOWER PETAL
Outer row–3 strands 3078
Inner rows–3 strands 550

SIDE PETALS
Outer and second rows–blend 2 strands 746 and 1 strand 3078
Inner rows–3 strands 550

UPPER PETALS
All rows–blend 2 strands 902 and 1 strand 550 (or 3 strands 154)

MARKINGS
'V' mark–blend 2 strands 902 and 1 strand 550 (or 3 strands 154), straight stitches

Add a 'V' shaped mark to edge of lower petal, halfway around, with four or five small stitches. See embroidered sample

OUTLINE
Side and upper petals–1 strand 746, backstitch or outline stitch
Lower petal–1 strand 550, backstitch or outline stitch

CENTRE
Throat–2 strands 444, straight stitches
Work quite a big throat stitching well down into the lower petal
Sides–2 strands 746, straight stitches or bullion stitches
Stigma–3 strands 472, French knot

THREADS	PETALS			THROAT & CENTRE		
DMC	550	902	3078	444	472	746
Finca	2635*	2171	1214	1227	4799	1211
Appleton's	456	149	841	553	251A	871
Soie d'Alger	3316	4625	2121	536	2123	crème

For Jenny Bradford

25. Purple & Cream Pansy

THREADS

DMC 154, 310, 445, 550, 3078,
(472, 746, 972)
Work petals for pansy with long and
short stitch leaving the centre triangle
and space for throat free of stitches.

LOWER PETAL

Outer row–3 strands 550, work the long
stitches shorter than usual

Second row–3 strands 445

Inner rows–3 strands 550 (or blend
2 strands 550 and 1 strand 938)

SIDE PETALS

Outer row–3 strands 550, work the long
stitches shorter than usual

Second and third rows–3 strands 3078

Inner rows–3 strands 550

UPPER PETALS

All rows–3 strands 154

STRIPES

Lower petal–1 strand 310, straight stitches

Add several long stripes to lower petal

Side petals–1 strand 154, straight stitches

Add a few stripes over inner rows

OUTLINE

Upper petals–1 strand 550, backstitch or
outline stitch

Lower and side petals–1 strand 550
and also 1 strand 3078, backstitch or
outline stitch

Work the outline to match the outer row
of stitches

CENTRE

Throat–2 strands 972, straight stitches

This pansy has quite a pronounced throat
so make the stitches longer than usual

Sides–2 strands 746, straight stitches
or bullion stitches

Stigma–3 strands 472, French knot

THREADS	PETALS					THROAT & CENTRE		
DMC	154	310	445	550	3078	472	746	972
Finca	—	0007	1217	2635*	1214	4799	1211	1232
Appleton's	607	993	551	456	841	251A	871	555
Soie d'Alger	5116	noir	2523	3316	2121	2123	crème	545

For Gini Hole
For Cathy Crawford

26. Deep Lavender & Dark Brown Pansy

THREADS

DMC 327, 829, 938, 3740,
(444, 472, 746)
Work petals for pansy with long and short stitch leaving the centre triangle and space for throat free of stitches.

LOWER PETAL

Outer row–blend 2 strands 829 and 1 strand 3740
Inner rows–3 strands 938

SIDE PETALS

Outer and second rows–blend 2 strands 829 and 1 strand 3740
Inner rows–3 strands 938

UPPER PETALS

All rows–3 strands 3740
Stripes–1 strand 829, straight stitches
Add several stripes to top petals

OUTLINE

All petals–1 strand 327, backstitch or outline stitch

CENTRE

Throat–2 strands 444, straight stitches
Sides–2 strands 746, straight stitches or bullion stitches
Stigma–3 strands 472, French knot

THREADS	PETALS				THROAT & CENTRE		
DMC	327	829	938	3740	444	472	746
Finca	—	7073	8171	8620*	1227	4799	1211
Appleton's	455	914	582	605	553	251A	871
Soie d'Alger	3315	526	4132	4635*	536	2123	crème

For Sally Milner

27. Antique Purple & Brown Pansy

THREADS

DMC 327, 829, 938, (444, 472, 746)
Work petals for pansy with long
and short stitch leaving the centre
triangle and space for throat free
of stitches.

LOWER PETAL

Outer row–3 strands 327

Second row–3 strands 829

Inner rows–3 strands 938

SIDE PETALS

Outer row–3 strands 327

Second and third row–3 strands 829

Inner rows–3 strands 938

UPPER PETALS

All rows–3 strands 327

OUTLINE

All petals–1 strand 327, backstitch
or outline stitch

CENTRE

Throat–2 strands 444, straight stitches

Sides–2 strands 746, straight stitches
or bullion stitches

Stigma–3 strands 472, French knot

THREADS	PETALS			THROAT & CENTRE		
DMC	327	829	938	444	472	746
Finca	—	7073	8171	1227	4799	1211
Appleton's	455	914	582	553	251A	871
Soie d'Alger	3315	526	4132	536	2123	crème

For Jane Fisk

28. Purple Pansy

THREADS

DMC 310, 550, (444, 472, 746)
Work petals for pansy with long
and short stitch leaving the centre
triangle and space for throat free
of stitches.

ALL PETALS

All rows–3 strands 550

STRIPES

1 strand 310, straight stitch

Add about eleven quite long stripes to
lower petal, several to side petals and
a few shorter ones to upper petals

OUTLINE

All petals–1 strand 550, backstitch or
outline stitch

CENTRE

Throat–2 strands 444, straight stitches

This pansy has quite a pronounced
throat so make the stitches a little
longer than usual

Sides–2 strands 746, straight stitches
or bullion stitches

Stigma–3 strands 472, French knot

THREADS	PETALS		THROAT & CENTRE		
DMC	310	550	444	472	746
Finca	0007	2635*	1227	4799	1211
Appleton's	993	456	553	251A	871
Soie d'Alger	noir	3316	536	2123	crème

For Gillian Morrison
For Chris Faulks

29. Dark Grape Pansy

This pansy has quite small flowers.

THREAD

DMC 550, 902, 3834, (444, 472, 746)
Work petals for pansy with long
and short stitch leaving the centre
triangle and space for throat free
of stitches.

LOWER PETAL

Outer and second rows–3 strands
3834 (or 327)
Inner rows–blend 2 strands 902
and 1 strand 550

SIDE PETALS

Outer, second and third rows–3
strands 3834 (or 327)

Inner row–blend 2 strands 902
and 1 strand 550

UPPER PETALS

All rows–3 strands 3834 (or 327)

OUTLINE

All petals–1 strand 3834, backstitch
or outline stitch

CENTRE

Throat–2 strands 444, straight stitches

Sides–2 strands 746, straight stitches
or bullion stitches

Stigma–3 strands 472, French knot

THREADS	PETALS			THROAT & CENTRE		
DMC	550	902	3834	444	472	746
Finca	2635*	2171	2635*	1227	4799	1211
Appleton's	456	149	606	553	251A	871
Soie d'Alger	3316	4625	4646	536	2123	crème

For Catherine Rich

30. Purple & Mauve Pansy

THREADS

DMC 208, 211, 310, 550, 3743,
(208, 444, 472)

Work petals for pansy with long
and short stitch leaving the centre
triangle and space for throat free of
stitches. Please note that in the
centre of this pansy the sides of
triangle are worked with 208.

LOWER PETAL

All rows–3 strands 550

SIDE PETALS

All rows–3 strands 550

UPPER PETALS

Outer and second rows–2 strands 211
and 1 strand 3743
Inner row–3 strands 208

MARKINGS

'V' mark–2 or 3 strands 208,
straight stitches

Add 'V' shaped mark halfway around
the edge of lower petal with four
or five small stitches.
See embroidered sample.

STRIPES

1 strand 310, straight stitches

Add about seven long stripes to lower
petal and four or five shorter ones to
side petals

OUTLINE

Lower and side petals–1 strand 550,
backstitch or outline stitch

Upper petals–1 strand 211, backstitch
or outline stitch

CENTRE

Throat–2 strands 444, straight stitches

Sides–2 strands 208, straight stitches
or bullion stitches

Stigma–3 strands 472, French knot

THREADS	PETALS				THROAT & CENTRE		
DMC	211	310	550	3743	208	444	472
Finca	2687	0007	2635*	8599	2615	1227	4799
Appleton's	884	993	456	891	454	553	251A
Soie d'Alger	3322*	noir	3316	3332	1334	536	2123

For Tilly Saunders

31. Shades of Purple Pansy

THREADS
DMC 208, 550, (444, 472, 746)
Work petals for pansy with long and short stitch leaving the centre triangle and space for throat free of stitches.

LOWER PETAL
Outer row—3 strands 208
Inner rows—3 strands 550

SIDE PETALS
Outer and second row—3 strands 208
Inner rows—3 strands 550

UPPER PETALS
All rows—3 strands 208

OUTLINE
All petals—1 strand 550, backstitch or outline stitch

CENTRE
Throat—2 strands 444, straight stitches
Sides—2 strands 746, straight stitches or bullion stitches
Stigma—3 strands 472, French knot

THREADS	PETALS		THROAT & CENTRE		
DMC	208	550	444	472	746
Finca	2615	2635*	1227	4799	1211
Appleton's	454	456	553	251A	871
Soie d'Alger	1334	3316	536	2123	crème

For Carmen Garcia

32. Shades of Lavender Pansy

This pansy has fairly large flowers.

THREADS

DMC 208, 209, 550, 3837
(444, 472, 746)
Work petals for pansy with long
and short stitch leaving the centre
triangle and space for throat free
of stitches.

LOWER PETAL AND SIDE PETALS

All rows—3 strands 3837

UPPER PETALS

All rows—blend 2 strands 209 and
1 strand 208

STRIPES

Lower and side petals—1 strand 550

Add several long stripes to lower petal
and four or five shorter ones
to side petals

OUTLINE

Lower and side petals—1 strand 3837,
backstitch or outline stitch

Upper petals—1 strand 208, backstitch
or outline stitch

CENTRE

Throat—2 strands 444, straight stitches

Work quite a big throat well down
into the lower petal

Sides—2 strands 746, straight stitches
or bullion stitches

Stigma—3 strands 472, French knot

THREADS	PETALS				THROAT & CENTRE		
DMC	208	209	550	3837	444	472	746
Finca	2615	2606	2635*	2627	1227	4799	1211
Appleton's	454	451	456	453	553	251A	871
Soie d'Alger	1334	3313	3316	1324	536	2123	crème

For Marion Trezise

33. Mauve & Purple Pansy

THREADS

DMC 316, 550, 3041, (472, 746, 972)
Work petals for pansy with long and
short stitch leaving the centre triangle
and space for throat free of stitches.

LOWER PETAL

Outer row–blend 2 strands 316 and
1 strand 3041, (or 2 strands 3803 and
1 of 3740)
Inner rows–3 strands 550

SIDE PETALS

Outer row–blend 2 strands 316 and
1 strand 3041, (or 2 strands 3803 and
1 of 3740)
Inner rows–3 strands 550

UPPER PETALS

Outer row–3 strands 316
(or 3 strands 3803)
Inner rows–3 strands 550

OUTLINE

All petals–1 strand 316, (or 3803),
backstitch or outline stitch

CENTRE

Throat–2 strands 972, straight stitches
Sides–2 strands 746, straight stitches
or bullion stitches
Stigma–3 strands 472, French knot

THREADS	PETALS			THROAT & CENTRE		
DMC	316	550	3041	472	746	972
Finca	2110*	2635*	8620	4799	1211	1232
Appleton's	712	456	933	251A	871	555
Soie d'Alger	4634	3316	5113	2123	crème	545

For Ros Hodgkins

34. Pink & Dark Red Pansy

THREADS

DMC 814, 3727, (444, 472, 746)
Work petals for pansy with long and short stitch leaving the centre triangle and space for throat free of stitches.

LOWER PETAL

Outer row–3 strands 3727 (or blend 2 strands 3042 and 1 strand 3727)
Inner rows–3 strands 814

SIDE PETALS

Outer and second rows–3 strands 3727 (or blend 2 strands 3042 and 1 strand 3727)
Inner row–3 strands 814

UPPER PETALS

All rows–3 strands 3727 (or blend 2 strands 3042 and 1 strand 3727)

OUTLINE

All petals–1 strand 3727 (or 3042), backstitch or outline stitch

CENTRE

Throat–2 strands 444, straight stitches
Sides–2 strands 746, straight stitches or bullion stitches
Stigma–3 strands 472, French knot

Variation: threads for a mauve version of this pansy are in brackets. See example on book cover.

THREADS	PETALS		THROAT & CENTRE		
DMC	814	3727	444	472	746
Finca	2171	2098	1227	4799	1211
Appleton's	759	711	553	251A	871
Soie d'Alger	946	1311*	536	2123	crème

For Rosemary Mallett
For Lesley Sligar

35. Cream, Yellow, Pink & Purple Pansy

THREADS
DMC 316, 445, 550, 746, 938,
(444, 472, 746)
Work petals for pansy with long and
short stitch leaving the centre triangle
and space for throat free of stitches.

LOWER PETAL
Outer row–3 strands 445
Second row–3 strands 550
Inner row–blend 2 strands 550
and 1 strand 938

SIDE PETALS
Outer row–3 strands 746
Inner rows–3 strands 550

UPPER PETALS
Outer row–3 strands 746
Inner rows–3 strands 316

STRIPES
1 strand 550, straight stitches
Add three or four stripes to upper petals

'V' MARK
Lower petal–3 strands 316,
straight stitches
Work a small pink 'V' with four or
five small stitches to edge of petal,
halfway round

OUTLINE
Lower petal–1 strand 445, backstitch
or outline stitch
Side and upper petals–1 strand 746,
backstitch or outline stitch

CENTRE
Throat–2 strands 444, straight stitches
Sides–2 strands 746, straight stitches
or bullion stitches
Stigma–3 strands 472, French knot

THREADS	PETALS				THROAT & CENTRE		
DMC	316	445	550	938	444	472	746
Finca	2110*	1217	2635*	8171	1227	4799	1211
Appleton's	712	551	456	582	553	251A	871
Soie d'Alger	4634	2523	3316	4132	536	2123	crème

For Sue Bailey
For Sue Game

36. Shades of Pink, Yellow & Rust Pansy

THREADS

DMC 307, 316, 400, 778, 938, 3685, 3687, (472, 746, 972)

Work petals for pansy with long and short stitch leaving the centre triangle and space for throat free of stitches.

LOWER PETAL

Outer row–3 strands 307

Inner rows–3 strands 400

SIDE PETALS

Outer and second rows–3 strands 778

Inner rows–3 strands 3687

UPPER PETALS

All rows–3 strands 316

STRIPES

Lower petal–1 strand 938, straight stitches

Add several long stripes to lower petal

Side petals–1 strand 307 and 1 strand 3685, straight stitches

Add a few yellow stripes over second row of stitching and several long stripes with 3685 over inner rows

Upper petals–1 strand 3687, straight stitches

Add four or five stripes to inner row

MARKINGS

'V' mark on lower petal–3 strands 3687, straight stitches

Work a small pink 'V' with four or five small stitches to edge of petal, halfway round

OUTLINE

All petals–1 strand 316, backstitch or outline stitch

CENTRE

Throat–2 strands 972, straight stitches

Sides–2 strands 746, straight stitches or bullion stitches

Stigma–3 strands 472, French knot

THREADS	PETALS							THROAT & CENTRE		
DMC	307	316	400	778	938	3685	3687	472	746	972
Finca	1222	2110*	7656	2098	8171	2246	2240	4799	1211	1232
Appleton's	552*	712	479	711	582	758	145	251A	871	555
Soie d'Alger	535*	4634	4141	2941	4132	3026	3024	2123	crème	545

For Lynne Harlow

37. Yellow, Pink & Maroon Pansy

THREADS
DMC 221, 316, 726, (444, 472, 746)
Work petals for pansy with long and short stitch leaving the centre triangle and space for throat free of stitches.

LOWER PETAL
All rows–3 strands 221

SIDE PETALS
Outer row–3 strands 726
Second row–blend 2 strands 316 and 1 strand 726
Inner rows–3 strands 221

UPPER PETALS
Outer row–blend 2 strands 316 and 1 strand 726
Second and inner rows–3 strands 316

OUTLINE
Lower petals–1 strand 221, backstitch or outline stitch
Side and upper petals–1 strand 726, backstitch or outline stitch

CENTRE
Throat–2 strands 444, straight stitches
Sides–2 strands 746, straight stitches or bullion stitches
Stigma–3 strands 472, French knot

THREADS	PETALS			THROAT & CENTRE		
DMC	221	316	726	444	472	746
Finca	1996	2110*	1010*	1227	4799	1211
Appleton's	226	712	552	553	251A	871
Soie d'Alger	4624	4634	522	536	2123	crème

For Emma Pickens

38. Dusky Pink, Yellow & Maroon Pansy

THREADS

DMC 316, 726, 814, (444, 472, 746)

Work petals for pansy with long and short stitch leaving the centre triangle and space for throat free of stitches.

LOWER PETAL

Outer row–sides: 3 strands 726 and middle: 2 strands 316 and 1 strand 726

Work splashes of yellow for sides of petal and middle section with blended threads

Second and inner rows–3 strands 814

SIDE PETALS

Outer row–3 strands 316

Second row–2 strands 316 and 1 strand 726

Third row–3 strands 726, work this row with fairly short stitches

Inner row–3 strands 814

UPPER PETALS

All rows–3 strands 316

OUTLINE

Lower petal–1 strand 726, backstitch or outline stitch

Side and upper petals–1 strand 316, backstitch or outline stitch

CENTRE

Throat–2 strands 444, straight stitches

Sides–2 strands 746, straight stitches or bullion stitches

Stigma–3 strands 472, French knot

THREADS	PETALS			THROAT & CENTRE		
DMC	316	726	814	444	472	746
Finca	2110*	1010*	2171	1227	4799	1211
Appleton's	712	552	759	553	251A	871
Soie d'Alger	4634	522	946	536	2123	crème

For Gabrielle Donovan

39. Dusky Pink, Maroon & Purple Pansy

THREADS

DMC 223, 550, 902, 3726, (472, 746, 972)

Work petals for pansy with long and short stitch leaving the centre triangle and space for throat free of stitches.

LOWER PETAL

Outer row–blend 2 strands 223 and 1 strand 3726

Inner rows–3 strands 902

SIDE PETALS

Outer and second row–blend 2 strands 223 and 1 strand 3726

Inner row–3 strands 550

UPPER PETALS

All rows–blend 2 strands 3726 and 1 strand 223

OUTLINE

All petals–1 strand 3727, backstitch or outline stitch

CENTRE

Throat–2 strands 972, straight stitches or bullion stitches

Sides–2 strands 746, straight stitches or bullion stitches

Stigma–3 strands 472, French knot

THREADS	PETALS				THROAT & CENTRE		
DMC	223	550	902	3726	472	746	972
Finca	1981	2635*	2171	2110	4799	1211	1232
Appleton's	754	456	149	713	251A	871	555
Soie d'Alger	2932	3316	4625	4645	2123	crème	545

For Pam Arnott

40. Soft Pink, Lavender & Rust Pansy

THREADS

DMC 301, 327, 3041, 3727, 3856, (472, 746, 972)

Work petals for pansy with long and short stitch leaving the centre triangle and space for throat free of stitches.

LOWER PETAL

Outer row–blend 2 strands 3727 and 1 strand 3856

Second row–blend 2 strands 3856 and 1 strand 3727

Inner row–3 strands 301

SIDE PETALS

Outer row–3 strands 3727

Second row–blend 2 strands 3856 and 1 strand 3727

Inner row–3 strands 3041

UPPER PETALS

All rows–3 strands 3727

STRIPES

Lower and side petals–1 strand 327, straight stitch

Add a few stripes to lower petal and some shorter ones to the side petals

OUTLINE

All petals–1 strand 3727, backstitch or outline stitch

CENTRE

Throat–2 strands 972, straight stitches

Sides–2 strands 746, straight stitches or bullion stitches

Stigma–3 strands 472, French knot

Variation: for a faded version of this pansy use 778 instead of 3727

THREADS	PETALS					THROAT & CENTRE		
DMC	301	327	3041	3727	3856	472	746	972
Finca	7740	—	8620	2098	7720	4799	1211	1232
Appleton's	478	455	933	711	861	251A	871	555
Soie d'Alger	2616	3315	5113	1311*	2632	2123	crème	545

For Krystyna Koltun

41. Dusky Pink, Yellow & Dark Brown Pansy

THREADS

DMC 316, 444, 938, 3726,
(444, 472, 746)
Work petals for pansy with long
and short stitch leaving the centre
triangle and space for throat free
of stitches.

LOWER PETAL

Outer row–blend 2 strands 316
and 1 strand 3726
Second row–3 strands 444
Work the stitches in this row a little
shorter than usual
Inner rows–3 strands 938

SIDE PETALS

Outer and second rows–blend 2
strands 316 and 1 strand 3726
Third row–3 strands 444
Work the stitches in this row a little
shorter than usual
Inner row–3 strands 938

UPPER PETALS

All rows–blend 2 strands 316
and 1 strand 3726
Stripes–2 strands 444, straight stitches
Add a few stripes to inner row

OUTLINE

Lower and side petals–1 strand 444,
backstitch or outline stitch
Upper petals–1 strand 316, backstitch
or outline stitch

CENTRE

Throat–2 strands 444, straight stitches
Sides–2 strands 746, straight stitches
or bullion stitches
Stigma–3 strands 472, French knot

*Variation: for a darker version of
this pansy blend 2 strands 3726
and 1 strand 315*

THREADS	PETALS			THROAT & CENTRE		
DMC	316	938	3726	444	472	746
Finca	2110*	8171	2110	1227	4799	1211
Appleton's	712	582	713	553	251A	871
Soie d'Alger	4634	4132	4645	536	2123	crème

For Ruth Penny
For Jane Crisp

42. Pink, Yellow & Maroon Pansy

THREADS

DMC 223, 725, 902, 938, 3722,
(444, 472, 746)
Work petals for pansy with long
and short stitch leaving the centre
triangle and space for throat free
of stitches.

LOWER PETAL

Outer or outer and second row–
blend 2 strands 725 and 1 strand 223
Inner rows–blend 2 strands 902
and 1 strand 938

SIDE PETALS

Outer and second row–blend 2
strands 223 and 1 strand 725
Inner rows–3 strands 902

UPPER PETALS

All rows–3 strands 3722 (or 3721)
Stripes–1 strand 902, straight stitches

OUTLINE

All petals–1 strand 725, backstitch
or outline stitch

CENTRE

Throat–2 strands 444, straight stitches
Sides–2 strands 746, straight stitches
or bullion stitches
Stigma–3 strands 472, French knot

*Variation: to work a version of this
pansy when it is newly opened, stitch
upper petals with 3721. On embroidered
sample one petal is stitched with 3722
and the other with 3721*

THREADS	PETALS					THROAT & CENTRE		
DMC	223	725	902	938	3722	444	472	746
Finca	1981	1062	2171	8171	1984	1227	4799	1211
Appleton's	754	554	149	582	755	553	251A	871
Soie d'Alger	2932	522	4625	4132	—	536	2123	crème

For Elizabeth Johnson

43. Yellow, Pink & Maroon Pansy

THREADS

DMC 223, 444, 726, 902, 938,
(444, 472, 746)
Work petals for pansy with long and
short stitch leaving the centre triangle
and space for throat free of stitches.

LOWER PETAL

Outer row–blend 2 strands 444
and 1 strand 726
Inner rows–blend 2 strands 902
and 1 strand 938

SIDE PETALS

Outer and second rows–blend
2 strands 726 and 1 strand 444
Inner rows–3 strands 902

UPPER PETALS

All rows–3 strands 223
Stripes–1 strand 902, straight stitches
Add a few stripes to upper petals

PATCHES OF PINK

Lower and side petals–3 strands 223,
straight stitches
Add a few stitches for patches of pink
to edge of lower and side petals.
See embroidered sample.

OUTLINE

All petals–1 strand 726, backstitch
or outline stitch

CENTRE

Throat–2 strands 444, straight stitches
Sides–2 strands 746, straight stitches
or bullion stitches
Stigma–3 strands 472, French knot

THREADS	PETALS				THROAT & CENTRE		
DMC	223	726	902	938	444	472	746
Finca	1981	1010*	2171	8171	1227	4799	1211
Appleton's	754	552	149	582	553	251A	871
Soie d'Alger	2932	522	4625	4132	536	2123	crème

For Carol Smeaton
For Patti Mulcare

44. Gold, Pink & Tan Pansy

THREADS

DMC 223, 300, 725, (444, 472, 746)
Work petals for pansy with long
and short stitch leaving the centre
triangle and space for throat free
of stitches.

LOWER PETAL

All rows–3 strands 300

SIDE PETALS

Outer and second rows–3 strands 725

Inner rows–3 strands 300

UPPER PETALS

All rows–3 strands 223

STRIPES

1 strand 300 and also 1 strand 725,
straight stitches

Add just a few stripes in each colour
to upper petals

OUTLINE

All petals–1 strand 725, backstitch or
outline stitch

CENTRE

Throat–2 strands 444, straight stitches

Sides–2 strands 746, straight stitches
or bullion stitches

Stigma–3 strands 472, French knot

THREADS	PETALS			THROAT & CENTRE		
DMC	223	300	725	444	472	746
Finca	1981	7656*	1062	1227	4799	1211
Appleton's	754	767	554	553	251A	871
Soie d'Alger	2932	4215	522	536	2123	crème

For Nick Harper

45.Deep Pink & Dark Brown Pansy

THREADS

DMC 725, 726, 898, 938, 3722, (444, 472, 746)

Work petals for pansy with long and short stitch leaving the centre triangle and space for throat free of stitches.

LOWER PETAL

Outer row–blend 2 strands 3722 and 1 strand 725

Inner rows–3 strands 898

SIDE PETALS

Outer row–3 strands 3722

Second and inner rows–blend 2 strands 3722 and 1 strand 725

UPPER PETALS

All rows–3 strands 3722

STRIPES

Lower and side petals–1 strand 938, straight stitches

Add several long stripes to lower petal and several slightly shorter ones to side petals

OUTLINE

All petals–1 strand 726, backstitch or outline stitch

CENTRE

Throat–2 strands 444, straight stitches

This pansy has quite a pronounced throat so make the stitches a little longer than usual

Sides–2 strands 746, straight stitches or bullion stitches

Stigma–3 strands 472, French knot

THREADS	PETALS					THROAT & CENTRE		
DMC	725	726	898	938	3722	444	472	746
Finca	1062	1010*	8080	8171	1984	1227	4799	1211
Appleton's	554	552	305	582	755	553	251A	871
Soie d'Alger	522	522	4131	4132	—	536	2123	crème

For Christobel Hoeben
For Gerry Sluis

46. Terracotta, Dark Brown & Maroon Pansy

THREADS

DMC 356, 726, 902, 938, (444, 472, 746)
Work petals for pansy with long
and short stitch leaving the centre
triangle and space for throat free
of stitches.

LOWER PETAL

Outer row–blend 2 strands 356
and 1 strand 726
Inner rows–3 strands 938

SIDE PETALS

Outer and second row–blend
2 strands 356 and 1 strand 726
Inner rows–3 strands 902

UPPER PETALS

All rows–3 strands 356

OUTLINE

All petals–1 strand 726, backstitch
or outline stitch

CENTRE

Throat–2 strands 444, straight stitches
Sides–2 strands 746, straight stitches
or bullion stitches
Stigma 3 strands 472, French knot

*Variation: to work a paler version of
this pansy use 3778 instead of 356. See
example on book cover*

THREADS	PETALS				THROAT & CENTRE		
DMC	356	726	902	938	444	472	746
Finca	7813*	1010*	2171	8171	1227	4799	1211
Appleton's	206	552	149	582	553	251A	871
Soie d'Alger	4612	522	4625	4132	536	2123	crème

For Loreign Randall

47. Pink & Rust Pansy

THREADS

DMC 221, 316, 780, 902, 975, 3726, (472, 746, 972)

Work petals for pansy with long and short stitch leaving the centre triangle and space for throat free of stitches.

LOWER PETAL

Outer row–blend 2 strands 3726 and 1 strand 780

Inner rows–3 strands 975

SIDE PETALS

Outer row–3 strands 3726

Inner rows–blend 2 strands 3726 and 1 strand 780

UPPER PETALS

Outer row–blend 2 strands 3726 and 1 strand 316

Inner rows–3 strands 3726

STRIPES

Lower petal–1 strand 902, straight stitches

Side petals–1 strand 221, straight stitches

Stitch several long stripes to lower petal and several long stripes to side petals

OUTLINE

All petals–1 strand 316, backstitch or outline stitch

CENTRE

Throat–2 strands 972, straight stitches

Sides–2 strands 746, straight stitches or bullion stitches

Centre–3 strands 472, French knot

THREADS	PETALS						THROAT & CENTRE		
DMC	221	316	780	902	975	3726	472	746	972
Finca	1996	2110*	8072	2171	7656	2110	4799	1211	1232
Appleton's	226	712	766	149	767	713	251A	871	555
Soie d'Alger	4624	4634	4213	4625	4215	4645	2123	crème	545

For Judy Spence

48. Tan, Rust & Maroon Pansy

THREADS

DMC 400, 444, 780, 902, 918, 975, 3371, (444, 472, 746)

Work petals for pansy with long and short stitch leaving the centre triangle and space for throat free of stitches.

LOWER PETAL

Outer row–blend 2 strands 918 and 1 strand 975

Inner rows–3 strands 902

SIDE PETALS

Outer and second rows–3 strands 918

Inner rows–3 strands 902

UPPER PETALS

All rows–blend 2 strands 780 and 1 strand 400

STRIPES

1 strand 3371, straight stitches

Add a few long stripes to lower petal and a few shorter ones to side petals

OUTLINE

Lower petal–1 strand 400 and also 1 strand 444, backstitch or outline stitch

Work the middle section of edge using 400 and either side with 444.

Side and upper petals–1 strand 400, backstitch or outline stitch

CENTRE

Throat–2 strands 444, straight stitches

Sides–2 strands 746, straight stitches or bullion stitches

Stigma–3 strands 472, French knot

THREADS	PETALS						THROAT & CENTRE		
DMC	400	780	902	918	975	3371	444	472	746
Finca	7656	8072	2171	7656*	7656	8083	1227	4799	1211
Appleton's	479	766	149	724	767	587	553	251A	871
Soie d'Alger	4141	4213	4625	2626	4215	4146	536	2123	crème

For Gill Tidey

49. Tan Pansy

THREADS

DMC 400, 444, 780, 975, 3371, (444, 472, 746)

Work petals for pansy with long and short stitch leaving the centre triangle and space for throat free of stitches.

LOWER PETAL

All rows–blend 2 strands 400 and 1 strand 975

SIDE PETALS

All rows–blend 2 strands 400 and 1 strand 975

UPPER PETALS

All rows–blend 2 strands 400 and 1 strand 780

STRIPES

1 strand 3371, straight stitches

Add a few long branching stripes to lower and side petals

OUTLINE

Lower petal–1 strand 780 and also 1 strand 444, backstitch or outline stitch

Work the middle section of edge using 780 and either side with 444

Side and upper petals–1 strand 780, backstitch or outline stitch

CENTRE

Throat–2 strands 444, straight stitches

Sides–2 strands 746, straight stitches or bullion stitches

Stigma–3 strands 472, French knot

THREADS	PETALS				THROAT & CENTRE		
DMC	400	780	975	3371	444	472	746
Finca	7656	8072	7656	8083	1227	4799	1211
Appleton's	479	766	767	587	553	251A	871
Soie d'Alger	4141	4213	4215	4146	536	2123	crème

For Liane Needham

50. Rust, Tan & Dark Brown Pansy

THREADS

DMC 400, 444, 780, 938, 3371, (444, 472, 746)

Work petals for pansy with long and short stitch leaving the centre triangle and space for throat free of stitches.

LOWER PETAL

Outer row–3 strands 400

Inner rows–3 strands 938

SIDE PETALS

Outer and second rows– 3 strands 400

Inner rows–3 strands 938

UPPER PETALS

All rows–3 strands 780

STRIPES

1 strand 3371, straight stitches

Add a few long stripes to lower petal and a few shorter ones to side petals

OUTLINE

Lower petal–1 strand 780 and also 1 strand 444, backstitch or outline stitch

Work the middle section of edge using 780 and either side with 444

Side and upper petals–1 strand 780, backstitch or outline stitch

CENTRE

Throat–2 strands 444, straight stitches

Sides–2 strands 746, straight stitches or bullion stitches

Stigma–3 strands 472, French knot

THREADS	PETALS				THROAT & CENTRE		
DMC	400	780	938	3371	444	472	746
Finca	7656	8072	8171	8083	1227	4799	1211
Appleton's	479	766	582	587	553	251A	871
Soie d'Alger	4141	4213	4132	4146	536	2123	crème

For Robin Slaughter
For Janet Roche

51. Rich Rust & Dark Brown Pansy

THREADS

DMC 918, 938, (444, 472, 746)
Work petals for pansy with long
and short stitch leaving the centre
triangle and space for throat free
of stitches.

LOWER PETAL

Outer row–3 strands 918

Inner rows–3 strands 938

SIDE PETALS

Outer and second rows–3 strands 918

Inner rows–3 strands 938

UPPER PETALS

All rows–3 strands 918

OUTLINE

All petals–1 strand 918, backstitch
or outline stitch

CENTRE

Throat–2 strands 444, straight stitches

Sides–2 strands 746, straight stitches
or bullion stitches

Stigma–3 strands 472, French knot

THREADS	PETALS		THROAT & CENTRE		
DMC	918	938	444	472	746
Finca	7656*	8171	1227	4799	1211
Appleton's	724	582	553	251A	871
Soie d'Alger	2626	4132	536	2123	crème

For Sue Hall

52. Dark Rust & Black Brown Pansy

THREADS

DMC 221, 919, 3371, (444, 472, 746)
Work petals for pansy with long and short stitch leaving the centre triangle and space for throat free of stitches.

LOWER PETAL

Outer row–blend 2 strands 221 and 1 strand 919

Inner rows–3 strands 3371

SIDE PETALS

Outer and second rows–blend 2 strands 221 and 1 strand 919

Inner row–3 strands 3371

UPPER PETALS

All rows–blend 2 strands 919 and 1 strand 221

OUTLINE

All petals–1 strand 919, backstitch or outline stitch

CENTRE

Throat–2 strands 444, straight stitches

Sides–2 strands 746, straight stitches or bullion stitches

Stigma–3 strands 472, French knot

THREADS	PETALS			THROAT & CENTRE		
DMC	221	919	3371	444	472	746
Finca	1996	7580*	8083	1227	4799	1211
Appleton's	226	726	587	553	251A	871
Soie d'Alger	4624	616	4146	536	2123	crème

For Thea Maclean

53. Rust & Black Brown with Yellow Pansy

THREADS

DMC 444, 919, 938, (444, 472, 746)
Work petals for pansy with long and short stitch leaving the centre triangle and space for throat free of stitches.

LOWER PETAL

Outer row–3 strands 919

Stripes–1 strand 444, straight stitches

Add stripes to outer row

Inner rows–3 strands 938

SIDE PETALS

Outer row–3 strands 919

Stripes–1 strand 444, straight stitches

Add stripes to outer row

Inner rows–3 strands 938

UPPER PETALS

All rows–3 strands 919

OUTLINE

Lower and side petals–1 strand 444, backstitch or outline stitch

Upper petals–1 strand 919, backstitch or outline stitch

CENTRE

Throat–2 strands 444, straight stitches

Sides–2 strands 746, straight stitches or bullion stitches

Stigma–3 strands 472, French knot

THREADS	PETALS		THROAT & CENTRE		
DMC	919	938	444	472	746
Finca	7580*	8171	1227	4799	1211
Appleton's	726	582	553	251A	871
Soie d'Alger	616	4132	536	2123	crème

For Dianne Firth

54. Rust, Brown & Gold Pansy

THREADS

DMC 300, 301, 725, (444, 472, 746)
Work petals for pansy with long
and short stitch leaving the centre
triangle and space for throat free
of stitches.

LOWER PETAL

All rows–3 strands 300

SIDE PETALS

Outer and second rows–blend 2
strands 301 and 1 strand 725
Inner rows–3 strands 300

UPPER PETALS

All rows–3 strands 301
Stripes–1 strand 300, straight stitches
Add a few stripes to inner rows

OUTLINE

Lower petal–1 strand 300, backstitch
or outline stitch

Side and upper petals–1 strand 725,
backstitch or outline stitch

CENTRE

Throat–2 strands 444, straight stitches
Sides–2 strands 746, straight stitches
or bullion stitches
Stigma–3 strands 472, French knot

THREADS	PETALS			THROAT & CENTRE		
DMC	300	301	725	444	472	746
Finca	7656*	7740	1062	1227	4799	1211
Appleton's	767	478	554	553	251A	871
Soie d'Alger	4215	2616	522	536	2123	crème

For Diana Primrose

55. Striped Rust & Yellow with Brown Pansy

THREADS

DMC 301, 444, 920, 3371, 3857,
(444, 472, 746)

Work petals for pansy with long and short stitch leaving the centre triangle and space for throat free of stitches.

LOWER PETAL

Outer row—3 strands 920, and also a blend of 2 strands 444 and 1 strand 301

Work several stitches for middle section with 920 and complete row on either side with the blended threads

Inner rows—3 strands 3857

SIDE PETALS

Outer row—blend 2 strands 920 and 1 strand 444

Second row—3 strands 444

Inner rows—3 strands 3857

UPPER PETALS

Outer row—blend 2 strands 301 and 1 strand 444

Inner rows—blend 2 strands 301 and 1 strand 920

STRIPES

Lower and side petals—1 strand 3371, straight stitches

Add a few stripes to lower petal and some shorter ones to the side petals

OUTLINE

All petals—1 strand 444, backstitch or outline stitch

CENTRE

Throat—2 strands 444, straight stitches

Sides—2 strands 746, straight stitches or bullion stitches

Stigma—3 strands 472, French knot

THREADS	PETALS				THROAT & CENTRE		
DMC	301	920	3371	3857	444	472	746
Finca	7740	7580	8083	7656*	1227	4799	1211
Appleton's	478	478	587	127	553	251A	871
Soie d'Alger	2616	2625	4146	4615	536	2123	crème

For Geoffrey Brooks

56. Striped Tan & Gold with Dark Brown Pansy

THREADS

DMC 301, 444, 725, 780, 938, (444, 472, 746)
Work petals for pansy with long and short stitch leaving the centre triangle and space for throat free of stitches.

LOWER PETAL

Outer row–blend 2 strands 301 and 1 strand 725

Inner rows–3 strands 938

SIDE PETALS

Outer row–blend 1 strand each 444, 725 and 301

Second row–3 strands 301

Inner rows–3 strands 938

UPPER PETALS

Outer row–blend 2 strands 725 and 1 strand 780

Inner rows–3 strands 780

OUTLINE

All petals–1 strand 444, backstitch or outline stitch

CENTRE

Throat–2 strands 444, straight stitches

Sides–2 strands 746, straight stitches or bullion stitches

Stigma–3 strands 472, French knot

THREADS	PETALS				THROAT & CENTRE		
DMC	301	725	780	938	444	472	746
Finca	7740	1062	8072	8171	1227	4799	1211
Appleton's	478	554	766	582	553	251A	871
Soie d'Alger	2616	522	4213	4132	536	2123	crème

For Juleen High
For Gail Lubbock

57. Yellow, Rust & Brown Pansy

THREADS

DMC 301, 444, 938, (444, 472, 746)
Work petals for pansy with long
and short stitch leaving the centre
triangle and space for throat free
of stitches.

LOWER PETAL

Outer row–3 strands 444
Inner rows–3 strands 938

SIDE PETALS

Outer row and second rows–
3 strands 444
Stripes–1 strand 301
Add stripes to outer rows
Inner rows–3 strands 938

UPPER PETALS

All rows–3 strands 301

OUTLINE

All petals–1 strand 444, backstitch
or outline stitch

CENTRE

Throat–2 strands 444, straight stitches
Sides–2 strands 746, straight stitches
or bullion stitches
Stigma–3 strands 472, French knot

*Variation:for a version of this pansy
when it is newly opened use 3776
instead of 301. See example on
book cover*

THREADS	PETALS		THROAT & CENTRE		
DMC	301	938	444	472	746
Finca	7740	8171	1227	4799	1211
Appleton's	478	582	553	251A	871
Soie d'Alger	2616	4132	536	2123	crème

For Ros McLusky

58. Yellow & Rust Pansy

This pansy has quite small flowers.

THREADS

DMC 444, 918, 3371, (444, 472, 746)
Work petals for pansy with long
and short stitch leaving the centre
triangle and space for throat free
of stitches.

LOWER PETAL

All rows–3 strands 444

SIDE PETALS

All rows–3 strands 444

UPPER PETALS

All rows–3 strands 918

MARKINGS

'V' mark on lower petal–3 strands 918,
straight stitches

Add a small rust mark to edge of
petal, halfway round, with three
small stitches

STRIPES

Lower and side petals–1 strand 3371,
straight stitches

Add several fairly short stripes
to lower petal and four or five to
side petals

OUTLINE

All petals–1 strand 444, backstitch
or outline stitch

CENTRE

Throat–2 strands 444, straight stitches

Sides–2 strands 746, straight stitches
or bullion stitches

Stigma–3 strands 472, French knot

*Variation: stripes could be worked with
902 instead of 3371*

THREADS	PETALS		THROAT & CENTRE		
DMC	918	3371	444	472	746
Finca	7656*	8083	1227	4799	1211
Appleton's	724	587	553	251A	871
Soie d'Alger	2626	4146	536	2123	crème

For Lorraine Freney

59. Mandarin Pansy

THREADS

DMC 741, 742, 3371, 3853, (472, 743, 746)
Work petals for pansy with long
and short stitch leaving the centre
triangle and space for throat free
of stitches.

LOWER PETAL

Outer row–blend 2 strands 742
and 1 strand 741
Inner rows–3 strands 3853

SIDE PETALS

Outer row–3 strands 742
Inner rows–blend 2 strands 742
and 1 strand 741

UPPER PETALS

All rows–3 strands 742

STRIPES

1 strand 3371, straight stitch
Add several long stripes to lower
petal and four to each side petal

OUTLINE

All petals–1 strand 742, backstitch
or outline stitch

CENTRE

Throat–2 strands 444, straight stitches
Sides–2 strands 746, straight stitches
or bullion stitches
Stigma–3 strands 472, French knot

*Variation: this pansy can be worked
without the stripes*

THREADS	PETALS				THROAT & CENTRE		
DMC	741	742	3371	3853	472	743	746
Finca	1152	1140	8083	7726	4799	1062	1211
Appleton's	556	555	587	557	251A	473	871
Soie d'Alger	624	545	4146	612	2123	522	crème

For Bernadette Cumper
For Betty McIntosh

60. Orange & Black Brown Pansy

THREADS
DMC 741, 742, 3371, 3853, (472, 741, 746)
Work petals for pansy with long
and short stitch leaving the centre
triangle and space for throat free
of stitches.

LOWER PETAL
Outer, second and third row–blend
2 strands 3853 and 1 strand 741
Work the third row of stitches shorter
than usual just filling the spaces
between stitches of the previous row
Inner row–3 strands 3371

SIDE PETALS
Outer, second and third rows–blend
2 strands 3853 and 1 strand 741
Work the third row of stitches shorter
than usual just filling the spaces
between stitches of the previous row
Inner row–3 strands 3371

UPPER PETALS
All rows–blend 2 strands 742
and 1 strand 741

OUTLINE
All petals–1 strand 741, backstitch
or outline stitch

CENTRE
Throat–2 strands 444, straight stitches
Sides–2 strands 746, straight stitches
or bullion stitches
Stigma–3 strands 472, French knot

THREADS	PETALS			THROAT & CENTRE		
DMC	742	3371	3853	472	741	746
Finca	1140	8083	7726	4799	1152	1211
Appleton's	555	587	557	251A	556	871
Soie d'Alger	545	4146	612	2123	624	crème

For Allyson Hamilton

61. Orange, Purple & Black Brown Pansy

THREADS

DMC 550, 741, 3371, 3854, (472, 741, 746)
Work petals for pansy with long
and short stitch leaving the centre
triangle and space for throat free
of stitches.

LOWER PETAL

Outer and second row—3 strands 741

Inner row—3 strands 3371

SIDE PETALS

Outer and second rows—blend
2 strands 741 and 1 strand 3854

Inner row—3 strands 3371

UPPER PETALS

All rows—3 strands 550

OUTLINE

All petals—1 strand 3854, backstitch
or outline stitch

CENTRE

Throat—2 strands 741, straight stitches

Sides—2 strands 746, straight stitches
or bullion stitches

Stigma—3 strands 472, French knot

THREADS	PETALS			THROAT & CENTRE		
DMC	550	3371	3854	472	741	746
Finca	2635*	8083	7726	4799	1152	1211
Appleton's	456	587	861*	251A	556	871
Soie d'Alger	3316	4146	2614	2123	624	crème

For Wendy May
For Wendy Kirby

62. Purple & Orange Pansy 'The Joker'

THREADS

DMC 327, 550, 741, 3853, 3854, (472, 741, 746)

Work petals for pansy with long and short stitch leaving the centre triangle and space for throat free of stitches.

LOWER PETAL

Outer and second row–3 strands 550

Inner rows–2 strands 741 and 1 strand 3853

SIDE PETALS

Outer and second row–3 strands 550

Inner rows–2 strands 741 and 1 strand 3853

UPPER PETALS

All rows–3 strands 550

STRIPES

Side and lower petals–1 strand 327, straight stitches

Add a few short stripes over inner rows (see sample)

OUTLINE

Lower and side petals–1 strand 550 and also 1 strand 3854, backstitch or outline stitch

Work most of the outline with 550 and just the upper part of petals with 3854. See embroidered sample

Upper petals–1 strand 550, backstitch or outline stitch

CENTRE

Throat–2 strands 741, straight stitches

Sides–2 strands 746, straight stitches or bullion stitches

Stigma–3 strands 472, French knot

THREADS	PETALS				THROAT & CENTRE		
DMC	327	550	3853	3854	472	741	746
Finca	—	2635*	7726	7726	4799	1152	1211
Appleton's	455	456	557	861*	251A	556	871
Soie d'Alger	3315	3316	612	2614	2123	624	crème

For Pam Burton

63. Deep Lavender, Apricot, Purple & Black Brown Pansy 'Harlequin'

THREADS

DMC 550, 742, 3371, 3740, 3854, (472, 741, 746)

Work petals for pansy with long and short stitch leaving the centre triangle and space for throat free of stitches.

LOWER PETAL

Outer row–3 strands 3740

Second row–2 strands 3854 and 1 strand 742

Inner row–3 strands 3371

SIDE PETALS

Outer row–3 strands 3740

Second row–2 strands 3854 and 1 strand 742

Inner row–3 strands 3371

UPPER PETALS

All rows–3 strands 550

OUTLINE

Side and lower petals–1 strand 3854, backstitch or outline stitch

Upper petals–1 strand 550, backstitch or outline stitch

CENTRE

Throat–2 strands 741, straight stitches

Sides–2 strands 746, straight stitches or bullion stitches

Stigma–3 strands 472, French knot

THREADS	PETALS					THROAT & CENTRE		
DMC	550	742	3371	3740	3854	472	741	746
Finca	2635*	1140	8083	8620*	7726	4799	1152	1211
Appleton's	456	555	587	605	861*	251A	556	871
Soie d'Alger	3316	545	4146	4635*	2614	2123	624	crème

For Antoinette Stojadinovic
For Amanda Knobel

64. Dark Red & Black Brown Pansy

THREADS

DMC 814, 3371, (444, 472, 746)
Work petals for pansy with long
and short stitch leaving the centre
triangle and space for throat free
of stitches.

LOWER PETAL

Outer and second row–3 strands 814
Inner row–3 strands 3371

SIDE PETALS

All rows–3 strands 814
Stripes–3 strands 3371
Add about five short stripes to inner
row of side petals

UPPER PETALS

All rows–3 strands 814

OUTLINE

All petals–1 strand 814, backstitch
or outline stitch

CENTRE

Throat–2 strands 444, straight stitches
Sides–2 strands 746, straight stitches
or bullion stitches
Stigma–3 strands 472, French knot

THREADS	PETALS		THROAT & CENTRE		
DMC	814	3371	444	472	746
Finca	2171	8083	1227	4799	1211
Appleton's	759	587	553	251A	871
Soie d'Alger	946	4146	536	2123	crème

For Peter Strang

65. Cherry & Navy Pansy

THREADS

DMC 939, 3685, (444, 472, 746)

Work petals for pansy with long and short stitch leaving the centre triangle and space for throat free of stitches.

LOWER PETAL

Outer and second row–3 strands 3685

Inner row–3 strands 939

SIDE PETALS

Outer and second rows–3 strands 3685

Inner row–3 strands 939

UPPER PETALS

All rows–3 strands 3685

OUTLINE

All petals–1 strand 3685, backstitch or outline stitch

CENTRE

Throat–2 strands 444, straight stitches

Sides–2 strands 746, straight stitches or bullion stitches

Stigma–3 strands 472, French knot

THREADS	PETALS		THROAT & CENTRE		
DMC	939	3685	444	472	746
Finca	3327	2246	1227	4799	1211
Appleton's	852	758	553	251A	871
Soie d'Alger	163	3026	536	2123	crème

For Cheryl Armstrong

66. Striped Maroon & Dark Red with Black Brown Pansy

THREADS

DMC 221, 814, 3371, (444, 472, 746)
Work petals for pansy with long and short stitch leaving the centre triangle and space for throat free of stitches.

LOWER PETAL

Outer row–blend 2 strands 814 and 1 strand 221

Inner rows–3 strands 3371

SIDE PETALS

Outer and second rows–blend 2 strands 814 and 1 strand 221

Inner row–3 strands 3371

UPPER PETALS

All rows–blend 2 strands 221 and 1 strand 814

OUTLINE

All petals–1 strand 221, backstitch or outline stitch

CENTRE

Throat–2 strands 444, straight stitches

Sides–2 strands 746, straight stitches or bullion stitches

Stigma–3 strands 472, French knot

THREADS	PETALS			THROAT & CENTRE		
DMC	221	814	3371	444	472	746
Finca	1996	2171	8083	1227	4799	1211
Appleton's	226	759	587	553	251A	871
Soie d'Alger	4624	946	4146	536	2123	crème

For Sophie Harper

67. Dusky Plum, Pink & Purple Pansy

THREADS

DMC 315, 550, 938, 3371, 3721, 3802, (472, 746, 972)

Work petals for pansy with long and short stitch leaving the centre triangle and space for throat free of stitches.

LOWER PETAL

Outer–3 strands 315

Second row–3 strands 3721

Inner rows–blend 2 strands 938 and 1 strand 550

SIDE PETALS

Outer and second rows–3 strands 315

Third row–3 strands 3721

Inner row–3 strands 550

UPPER PETALS

All rows–3 strands 3802

STRIPES

Side and lower petals–1 strand 3371, straight stitches

Add four or five short stripes to side petals and several longer ones to lower petal

OUTLINE

All petals–1 strand 315, backstitch or outline stitch

CENTRE

Throat–2 strands 972, straight stitches

Sides–2 strands 746, straight stitches or bullion stitches

Stigma–3 strands 472, French knot

THREADS	PETALS						THROAT & CENTRE		
DMC	315	550	938	3371	3721	3802	472	746	972
Finca	2123	2635*	8171	8083	1996	2123	4799	1211	1232
Appleton's	714	456	582	587	225	147	251A	871	555
Soie d'Alger	4645	3316	4132	4146	—	4646	2123	crème	545

For Rhondda Cleary
For Kay Blue

68. Raspberry Pansy

THREADS
DMC 154, 221, 3802, 3803, 3371,
(444, 472, 746)
Work petals for pansy with long
and short stitch leaving the centre
triangle and space for throat free
of stitches.

LOWER PETAL
Outer row–blend 2 strands 221 and
1 strand 3802
Inner rows–3 strands 221

SIDE PETALS
Outer and second rows–
3 strands 3802
Inner rows–blend 2 strands 221
and 1 strand 3802

UPPER PETALS
All rows–blend 2 strands 3803 and
1 strand 3802

STRIPES
Lower Petal–1 strand 3371,
straight stitches
Side petals–1 strand 154,
straight stitches
Add several long stripes to lower petal
and four or five to side petals

OUTLINE
All petals–1 strand 3803, backstitch
or outline stitch

CENTRE
Throat–2 strands 444, straight stitches
Sides–2 strands 746, straight stitches
or bullion stitches
Stigma–3 strands 472, French knot

THREADS	PETALS					THROAT & CENTRE		
DMC	154	221	3802	3803	3371	444	472	746
Finca	—	1996	2123	2246	8083	1227	4799	1211
Appleton's	607	226	147	146	587	553	251A	871
Soie d'Alger	5116	4624	4646	3026*	4146	536	2123	crème

For Dianna Budd

69. Shades of Pink Pansy

THREADS

DMC 221, 315, 355, 550, 902, 3721, 3722, (472, 746, 972)

Work petals for pansy with long and short stitch leaving the centre triangle and space for throat free of stitches.

LOWER PETAL

Outer row–2 strands 3722 and 1 strand 3721

Inner rows–3 strands 355

SIDE PETALS

Outer and second rows–2 strands 3722 and 1 strand 3721

Inner rows–3 strands 221

UPPER PETALS

Outer row–3 strands 315

Inner rows–3 strands 3722

STRIPES

Lower Petal–1 strand 902, straight stitches

Side petals–1 strand 550, straight stitches

Add several long stripes to lower petal and four or five shorter ones to side petals

OUTLINE

Lower and side petals–1 strand 3722, backstitch or outline stitch

Upper petals–1 strand 315, backstitch or outline stitch

CENTRE

Throat–2 strands 972, straight stitches

Sides–2 strands 746, straight stitches or bullion stitches

Stigma–3 strands 472, French knot

THREADS	PETALS							THROAT & CENTRE		
DMC	221	315	355	550	902	3721	3722	472	746	972
Finca	1996	2123	1996	2635*	2171	1996	1984	4799	1211	1232
Appleton's	226	714	208	456	149	225	755	251A	871	555
Soie d'Alger	4624	4645	616	3316	4625	—	—	2123	crème	545

For Charlotte Harper

70. Cerise & Purple Pansy

THREADS

DMC 550, 3803, (472, 746, 972)

Work petals for pansy with long and short stitch leaving the centre triangle and space for throat free of stitches.

LOWER PETAL

Outer and second row–3 strands 3803

Inner rows–3 strands 550

SIDE PETALS

Outer and second row–3 strands 3803

Inner rows–3 strands 550

UPPER PETALS

All rows–3 strands 3803

STRIPES

Lower & side petals–1 strand 550, straight stitches

Add several long stripes to lower petal & side petals

OUTLINE

All petals–1 strand 3803, backstitch or outline stitch

CENTRE

Throat–2 strands 972, straight stitches

Sides–2 strands 746, straight stitches or bullion stitches

Stigma–3 strands 472, French knot

THREADS	PETALS		THROAT & CENTRE		
DMC	550	3803	472	746	972
Finca	2635*	2246	4799	1211	1232
Appleton's	456	146	251A	871	555
Soie d'Alger	3316	3026*	2123	crème	545

For Lois Kinsman

71. Rose Pink & Maroon Pansy

THREADS

DMC 902, 3350, (444, 472, 746)
Work petals for pansy with long
and short stitch leaving the centre
triangle and space for throat free
of stitches.

LOWER PETAL

Outer row–3 strands 3350

Inner rows–3 strands 902

SIDE PETALS

Outer and second row–3 strands 3350

Inner rows–3 strands 902

UPPER PETALS

All rows–3 strands 3350

OUTLINE

All petals–1 strand 3350 or 902,
backstitch or outline stitch

CENTRE

Throat–2 strands 444, straight stitches

Sides–2 strands 746, straight stitches
or bullion stitches

Stigma–3 strands 472, French knot

THREADS	PETALS		THROAT & CENTRE		
DMC	902	3350	444	472	746
Finca	2171	2165	1227	4799	1211
Appleton's	149	757	553	251A	871
Soie d'Alger	4625	3025	536	2123	crème

For Rita Crawford

72. Maroon, Yellow & Dark Brown Pansy

THREADS
DMC 221, 444, 814, 938, (444, 472, 746)
Work petals for pansy with long and short stitch leaving the centre triangle and space for throat free of stitches.

LOWER PETAL
Outer row–3 strands 221
Second row–3 strands 444
Inner rows–3 strands 938

SIDE PETALS
Outer row–3 strands 221
Second and third row–3 strands 444
Inner row–3 strands 938

UPPER PETALS
All rows–3 strands 814

STRIPES
Lower and side petals–1 strand 444, straight stitches
Add a feathering of yellow stripes to outer row

OUTLINE
All petals–1 strand 814, backstitch or outline stitch

CENTRE
Throat–2 strands 444, straight stitches
Sides–2 strands 746, straight stitches or bullion stitches
Stigma–3 strands 472, French knot

THREADS	PETALS			THROAT & CENTRE		
DMC	221	814	938	444	472	746
Finca	1996	2171	8171	1227	4799	1211
Appleton's	226	759	582	553	251A	871
Soie d'Alger	4624	946	4132	536	2123	crème

For Bill Douglas

73. Bright Plum, Lemon & Purple Pansy

THREADS

DMC 307, 445, 550, 814, 902, 915, 3371, (472, 746, 972)

Work petals for pansy with long and short stitch leaving the centre triangle and space for throat free of stitches.

LOWER PETAL

Outer row—blend 2 strands 915 and 1 strand 814, work the long stitches shorter than usual

Second row—3 strands 307

Inner row—3 strands 902

SIDE PETALS

Outer row—blend 2 strands 915 and 1 strand 814, work the long stitches shorter than usual

Second and third rows—3 strands 445

Inner row—3 strands 550

UPPER PETALS

All rows—blend 2 strands 915 and 1 strand 814

STRIPES

Lower petal—1 strand 3371, straight stitches

Add several long stripes to lower petal working them from the centre and over the throat

OUTLINE

Side and lower petals—1 strand 445, backstitch or outline stitch

Upper petals—1 strand 915, backstitch or outline stitch

CENTRE

Throat—2 strands 972, straight stitches

This pansy has quite a pronounced throat so make the stitches a little longer than usual

Sides—2 strands 746, straight stitches or bullion stitches

Stigma—3 strands 472, French knot

THREADS	PETALS							THROAT & CENTRE		
DMC	307	445	550	814	902	915	3371	472	746	972
Finca	1222	1217	2635*	2171	2171	2415	8083	4799	1211	1232
Appleton's	552*	551	456	759	149	805	587	251A	871	555
Soie d'Alger	535*	2523	3316	946	4625	3026	4146	2123	crème	545

For Andrew Sikorski

74. Old Gold, Yellow & Dark Brown Pansy 'Heirloom'

THREADS

DMC 370, 444, 734, 834, 938, 3041, (472, 746, 972)

Work petals for pansy with long and short stitch leaving the centre triangle and space for throat free of stitches.

LOWER PETAL

Outer row–blend 2 strands 370 and 1 strand 734

Second row–3 strands 444

Inner row–3 strands 938

SIDE PETALS

Outer and second rows–blend 2 strands 370 and 1 strand 734

Third row–3 strands 444–work these stitches a little shorter than usual

Inner row–3 strands 938

UPPER PETALS

Outer and second rows–blend 2 strands 834 and 1 strand 734

Inner row–3 strands of 3041

Work a few stitches for final row adding a touch of lavender

OUTLINE

All petals–1 strand 734, backstitch or outline stitch

CENTRE

Throat–2 strands 972, straight stitches

This pansy has quite a pronounced throat so make the stitches a little longer than usual

Sides–2 strands 746, straight stitches or bullion stitches

Stigma–3 strands 472, French knot

THREADS	PETALS						THROAT & CENTRE		
DMC	370	444	734	834	938	3041	472	746	972
Finca	7318	1227	5224*	7046	8171	8620	4799	1211	1232
Appleton's	334	553	241	855	582	933	251A	871	555
Soie d'Alger	2212	536	2211	2233	4132	5113	2123	crème	545

For Anna Quach

75. Old Gold & Brown Pansy 'Heirloom'

THREADS

DMC 300, 370, 444, 734, 938, 3041, 3046, (472, 746, 972)

Work petals for pansy with long and short stitch leaving the centre triangle and space for throat free of stitches.

LOWER PETAL

Outer row–blend 2 strands 370 and 1 strand 734

Inner rows–2 strands 300 and 1 strand 938

SIDE PETALS

Outer and second rows–blend 2 strands 370 and 1 strand 734

Third row–3 strands 444, straight stitch

Inner rows–2 strands 300 and 1 strand 938

MARKINGS

Streaks–3 strands 444, straight stitches

Add streaks with a couple of stitches to lower petal, either side of centre. Do this at the same time as third row of side petals. See embroidered sample

UPPER PETALS

Outer and second rows–blend 2 strands 3046 and 1 strand 734

Inner row–3 strands of 3041

Work a few stitches for final row adding a touch of lavender

OUTLINE

All petals–1 strand 734, backstitch or outline stitch

CENTRE

Throat and streaks- 2 strands 972, straight stitches

Sides–2 strands 746, straight stitches or bullion stitches

Stigma–3 strands 472, French knot

THREADS	PETALS							THROAT & CENTRE		
DMC	300	370	444	734	938	3041	3046	472	746	972
Finca	7656*	7318	1227	5224*	8171	8620	7225	4799	1211	1232
Appleton's	767	334	553	241	582	933	331	251A	871	555
Soie d'Alger	4215	2212	536	2211	4132	5113	2141	2123	crème	545

For Karen Ramage

76. Muted Browns Pansy 'Heirloom'

Work petals for pansy with long and short stitch leaving the centre triangle and space for throat free of stitches.

THREADS

DMC 327, 371, 444, 550, 829, 3042, 3371, 3740, (444, 472, 746)

LOWER PETAL

Outer row–blend 2 strands 829 and 1 strand 3740

Inner rows–blend 2 strands 3371 and 1 strand 550

SIDE PETALS

Outer row–blend 2 strands 371 and 1 strand 3042

Second row–blend 2 strands 829 and 1 strand 3740

Inner rows–blend 2 strands 3371 and 1 strand 550

UPPER PETALS

All rows–2 strands 371 and 1 strand 3042

If desired work an inner row with blend 2 strands 327 and 1 strand 3740

MARKINGS

Streaks and flecks–2 strands 444, straight stitches

Add streaks with a couple of stitches to lower petal, either side of centre. Work flecks with small stitches to inner rows of side petals. Work at the same time as pansy throat.

STRIPES

1 strand 550, straight stitches

Add a few stripes to lower and side petals

OUTLINE

Lower petal–1 strand 3740, backstitch or outline stitch

Side and upper petals–1 strand 3042, backstitch or outline stitch

CENTRE

Throat–2 strands 444, straight stitches

Sides–2 strands 746, straight stitches or bullion stitches

Stigma–3 strands 472, French knot

THREADS	PETALS							THROAT & CENTRE		
DMC	327	371	550	829	3042	3371	3740	444	472	746
Finca	—	7318	2635*	7073	8605	8083	8620*	1227	4799	1211
Appleton's	455	333	456	914	603	587	605	553	251A	871
Soie d'Alger	3315	3833	3316	526	5112	4146	4635*	536	2123	crème

For June Humphrey

77. Muted Mauve & Gold with Black Brown Pansy 'Heirloom'

Work petals for pansy with long and short stitch leaving the centre triangle and space for throat free of stitches.

THREADS
DMC 370, 371, 444, 938, 3042, 3371, (444, 472, 746)

LOWER PETAL
Outer row–3 strands 370

Inner rows–blend 2 strands 3371 and 1 strand 938 (or 3 strands 3371)

SIDE PETALS
Outer row–blend 2 strands 370 and 1 strand 3042 (or 3 strands 370)

Second row–3 strands 370

Inner row–blend 2 strands 3371 and 1 strand 938 (or 3 strands 3371)

UPPER PETALS
Outer row–blend 2 strands 3042 and 1 strand 371 (or 3 strands 3042)

Inner rows–blend 2 strands 3042 and 1 strand 371

STRIPES
1 strand 938, straight stitch

Add a few long stripes to lower and side petals

OUTLINE
1 strand 3042, backstitch or outline stitch

CENTRE
Throat and streaks–2 strands 444, straight stitches

Add streaks with a couple of stitches to lower petal, either side of centre

Sides–2 strands 746, straight stitches or bullion stitches

Stigma–3 strands 472, French knot

THREADS	PETALS					THROAT & CENTRE		
DMC	370	371	938	3042	3371	444	472	746
Finca	7318	7318	8171	8605	8083	1227	4799	1211
Appleton's	334	333	582	603	587	553	251A	871
Soie d'Alger	2212	3833	4132	5112	4146	536	2123	crème

For Tricia Miles
For Lainie Lawson

78. Shades of Lavender & Purple Pansy 'Heirloom'

THREADS

DMC 208, 371, 444, 550, 3042, 3743, (444, 472, 746)

Work petals for pansy with long and short stitch leaving the centre triangle and space for throat free of stitches.

LOWER PETAL

Outer row–blend 2 strands 3042 and 1 strand 371

Second row–3 strands 550

Inner row and throat- 3 strands 444, straight stitches

Work throat at the same time as the inner row

SIDE PETALS

Outer and second row–blend 2 strands 3042 and 1 strand 371

Inner rows–3 strands 550

UPPER PETALS

All rows–3 strands 3743

Stripes–1 strand 208, straight stitch

Add a few stripes to inner row

OUTLINE

Upper petals–1 strand 3743, backstitch or outline stitch

Side and lower petals–1 strand 3042

CENTRE

(Throat–work at the same time as inner row)

Sides–2 strands 746, straight stitches or bullion stitches

Stigma–3 strands 472, French knot

THREADS	PETALS					THROAT & CENTRE		
DMC	208	371	550	3042	3743	444	472	746
Finca	2615	7318	2635*	8605	8599	1227	4799	1211
Appleton's	454	333	456	603	891	553	251A	871
Soie d'Alger	1334	3833	3316	5112	3332	536	2123	crème

For Sally Davis

79. Old Gold, Mauve, Purple & Dark Brown Pansy 'Heirloom'

THREADS

DMC 370, 444, 550, 938, 3041, 3042, 3046, (444, 472, 746)

Work petals for pansy with long and short stitch leaving the centre triangle and space for throat free of stitches.

LOWER PETAL

Outer row–blend 2 strands 370 and 1 strand 3042

Inner rows–3 strands 938

SIDE PETALS

Outer, second and third rows –3 strands 370

Inner row–3 strands 550

UPPER PETALS

Outer and second rows–blend 2 strands 3042 and 1 strand 3046

Inner row–3 strands 3041

OUTLINE

1 strand 3042, backstitch or outline stitch

CENTRE

Throat and streaks–2 strands 444, straight stitches

Add streaks with a couple of stitches to lower petal, either side of centre

Sides–2 strands 746, straight stitches or bullion stitches

Stigma–3 strands 472, French knot

THREADS	PETALS						THROAT & CENTRE		
DMC	370	550	938	3041	3042	3046	444	472	746
Finca	7318	2635*	8171	8620	8605	7225	1227	4799	1211
Appleton's	334	456	582	933	603	331	553	251A	871
Soie d'Alger	2212	3316	4132	5113	5112	2141	536	2123	crème

For Pam Atkinson

80. Antique Purple, Yellow, Mauve & Black Brown Pansy 'Heirloom'

THREADS

DMC 327, 444, 550, 726, 801, 3042, 3371, 3740, (444, 472, 746)

Work petals for pansy with long and short stitch leaving the centre triangle and space for throat free of stitches.

LOWER PETAL

Outer row–blend 2 strands 327 and 1 strand 801

Second row–3 strands 444

Inner row–3 strands 3371

SIDE PETALS

Outer row–3 strands 327

Second row–blend 2 strands 444 and 1 strand 726

Inner rows–blend 2 strands 3371 and 1 strand 550

UPPER PETALS

Outer row–3 strands 3042

Second and inner rows–3 strands 3740

Stripes–1 strand 327, straight stitches

OUTLINE

Lower petal–1 strand 444, backstitch or outline stitch

Upper and side petals–1 strand 3042, backstitch or outline stitch

CENTRE

Throat–2 strands 444, straight stitches

Sides–2 strands 746, straight stitches or bullion stitches

Stigma–3 strands 472, French knot

THREADS	PETALS							THROAT & CENTRE		
DMC	327	550	726	801	3042	3371	3740	444	472	746
Finca	—	2635*	1010*	8080	8605	8083	8620*	1227	4799	1211
Appleton's	455	456	552	304	603	587	605	553	251A	871
Soie d'Alger	3315	3316	522	4116	5112	4146	4635*	536	2123	crème

For Malcolm and Marianne Lampe

THREADS

DMC 327, 444, 550, 898, 938, 3041, 3042, 3046, (444, 472, 746)

Work petals for pansy with long and short stitch leaving the centre triangle and space for throat free of stitches.

LOWER PETAL

Outer and second row or just outer row–3 strands 898

Inner row or rows–3 strands 938

SIDE PETALS

Outer and second rows–3 strands 327

Third row–3 strands 444

Work these stitches a little shorter than usual

Inner row–3 strands 550

UPPER PETALS

Outer and second rows–blend 2 strands 3046 and 1 strand 3042

Inner row–3 strands 3041

OUTLINE

Lower and side petals–1 strand 444, backstitch or outline stitch

Upper petals–1 strand 3046, backstitch or outline stitch

CENTRE

Throat and streaks–2 strands 444, straight stitches

This pansy has quite a pronounced throat so make stitches a little longer than usual.

Add streaks with a stitch to outline on either side of centre. See embroidered sample

Sides–2 strands 746, straight stitches or bullion stitches

Stigma–3 strands 472, French knot

THREADS	PETALS							THROAT & CENTRE		
DMC	327	550	898	938	3041	3042	3046	444	472	746
Finca	—	2635*	8080	8171	8620	8605	7225	1227	4799	1211
Appleton's	455	456	305	582	933	603	331	553	251A	871
Soie d'Alger	3315	3316	4131	4132	5113	5112	2144	536	2123	crème

For Irene Ussenko

82. Purple, Violet & Black Pansy 'Heirloom'

THREADS

DMC 327, 333, 444, 550, 829, 3371,
(444, 472, 746)
Work petals for pansy with long and
short stitch leaving the centre triangle
and space for throat free of stitches.
Work the throat and streaks at the
same time.

LOWER PETAL

Outer row–3 strands 550
Second row–3 strands 829
Inner rows–3 strands 3371

SIDE PETALS

Outer and second rows–3 strands 550
Inner rows–3 strands 3371

UPPER PETALS

All rows–3 strands 333
Work a few stitches for final row
with 327 to add a touch of purple
to base of petals

STRIPES

1 strand 3371, straight stitch
Work several long stripes to lower
petal and to side petals

OUTLINE

All petals–1 strand 333, backstitch
or outline stitch

CENTRE

Throat and streaks–2 strands 444,
straight stitches
Add streaks with a stitch to outline
on either side of centre.
See embroidered sample
Sides–2 strands 746, straight stitches
or bullion stitches
Stigma–3 strands 472, French knot

THREADS	PETALS					THROAT & CENTRE		
DMC	327	333	550	829	3371	444	472	746
Finca	—	2699	2635*	7073	8083	1227	4799	1211
Appleton's	455	895	456	914	587	553	251A	871
Soie d'Alger	3315	1344	3316	526	4146	536	2123	crème

For Dianne Smith

83. Shades of Dusky Pink Pansy 'Masterpiece'

THREADS

DMC 223, 224, 315, 743, (472, 746, 972)
Work petals for pansy with long and short stitch leaving the centre triangle and space for throat free of stitches.

LOWER PETAL

Outer row–3 strands 223

Inner rows–blend 2 strands 224 and 1 strand 743

Upper and side petals

Outer row–3 strands 223

Inner rows–3 strands 224

STRIPES

Lower and side petals–1 strand 315, straight stitches

Add a few stripes to lower and side petals.

OUTLINE

All petals–1 strand 223, backstitch or outline stitch

CENTRE

Throat–2 strands 972, straight stitches

Sides–2 strands 746, straight stitches or bullion stitches

Stigma–3 strands 472, French knot

THREADS	PETALS				THROAT & CENTRE		
DMC	223	224	315	743	472	746	972
Finca	1981	7806	2123	1062	4799	1211	1232
Appleton's	754	753	714	473	251A	871	555
Soie d'Alger	2932	4621	4645	522	2123	crème	545

For Annette Rich

84. Shades of Pink Pansy 'Masterpiece'

THREADS

DMC 316, 550, 3687, (472, 746, 972)

Work petals for pansy with long and short stitch leaving the centre triangle and space for throat free of stitches.

LOWER PETAL

All rows–blend 2 strands 3687 and 1 strand 316

UPPER AND SIDE PETALS

Outer row–3 strands 316

Inner rows–blend 2 strands 316 and 1 strand 3687

STRIPES

All petals–1 strand 550, straight stitches

Work several long stripes to lower petal, about four short ones to side petals and a couple of very small stripes to upper petals

OUTLINE

All petals–1 strand 316, backstitch or outline stitch

CENTRE

Throat–2 strands 972, straight stitches

Sides–2 strands 746, straight stitches or bullion stitches

Stigma–3 strands 472, French knot

Variation: for a darker version of this pansy use 3803 instead of 3687

THREADS	PETALS			THROAT & CENTRE		
DMC	316	550	3687	472	746	972
Finca	2110*	2635*	2240	4799	1211	1232
Appleton's	712	456	145	251A	871	555
Soie d'Alger	4634	3316	3024	2123	crème	545

For Kerri West

85. Pale Pink & Gold Pansy 'Masterpiece'

THREADS
DMC 743, 778, 3726, 3774,
(472, 746, 972)
Work petals for pansy with long
and short stitch leaving the centre
triangle and space for throat free
of stitches.

LOWER PETAL
Outer row—3 strands 778
Inner rows—blend 2 strands 743
and 1 strand 3774

SIDE PETALS
Outer row—3 strands 778
Inner rows—3 strands 3774
Add 3 or 4 stitches to inner row with
blend 2 strands 743 and 1 strand 3774
(as used for lower petal)

UPPER PETALS
Outer row—3 strands 778
Inner rows—3 strands 3774

STRIPES
Lower and side petals—1 strand 3726,
straight stitches
Add a few stripes to lower and
side petals

OUTLINE
All petals—1 strand 778, backstitch
or outline stitch

CENTRE
Throat—2 strands 972, straight stitches
Sides—2 strands 746, straight stitches
or bullion stitches
Stigma—3 strands 472, French knot

*Variation: for a darker version of this
pansy use 3727 instead of 778*

THREADS	PETALS				THROAT & CENTRE		
DMC	743	778	3726	3774	472	746	972
Finca	1062	2098	2110	7933	4799	1211	1232
Appleton's	473	711	713	704	251A	871	555
Soie d'Alger	522	2941	4645	2911	2123	crème	545

For Steph Litchfield

86. Apricot, Lemon & Gold Pansy 'Masterpiece'

THREADS

DMC 743, 745, 945, 3772, (472, 746, 972)
Work petals for pansy with long and short stitch leaving the centre triangle and space for throat free of stitches.

LOWER PETAL

Outer row–3 strands 945
Inner rows–3 strands 743

SIDE PETALS

Outer row–blend 2 strands 945 and 1 strand 745
Inner rows–3 strands 745

UPPER PETALS

All rows–3 strands 945

STRIPES

Lower and side petals–1 strand 3772, straight stitches

Add a few stripes to lower petal and some shorter ones to the side petals.

OUTLINE

All petals–1 strand 945, backstitch or outline stitch

CENTRE

Throat–2 strands 972, straight stitches

Sides–2 strands 746, straight stitches or bullion stitches

Stigma–3 strands 472, French knot

THREADS	PETALS				THROAT & CENTRE		
DMC	743	745	945	3772	472	746	972
Finca	1062	1137	7936*	7944	4799	1211	1232
Appleton's	473	471	708	124	251A	871	555
Soie d'Alger	522	2531	2911	4613*	2123	crème	545

For Elisabeth Rundle

87. Peach, Cream & Gold Pansy 'Masterpiece'

THREADS

DMC 743, 745, 950, 951, 3772, (472, 746, 972)

Work petals for pansy with long and short stitch leaving the centre triangle and space for throat free of stitches.

LOWER PETAL

Outer row–3 strands 950

Inner rows–3 strands 743

SIDE PETALS

Outer row–3 strands 951

Inner rows–blend 2 strands 951 and 1 strand 745

UPPER PETALS

All rows–3 strands 950

STRIPES

Lower and side petals–1 strand 3772, straight stitches

Add a few stripes to lower petal and some shorter ones to the side petals

OUTLINE

All petals–1 strand 950, backstitch or outline stitch

CENTRE

Throat–2 strands 972, straight stitches

Sides–2 strands 746, straight stitches or bullion stitches

Stigma–3 strands 472, French knot

THREADS	PETALS					THROAT & CENTRE		
DMC	743	745	950	951	3772	472	746	972
Finca	1062	1137	7936	7933	7944	4799	1211	1232
Appleton's	473	471	202	705	124	251A	871	555
Soie d'Alger	522	2531	1011	641	4613*	2123	crème	545

For Vicky and Andrew Lampe

88. Soft Beige & Cream Pansy 'Masterpiece'

THREADS
DMC 3770, 3772, 3774, (472, 746, 972)
Work petals for pansy with long and short stitch leaving the centre triangle and space for throat free of stitches.

ALL PETALS
Outer row–3 strands 3774
Inner rows–3 strands 3770

STRIPES
Lower and side petals–1 strand 3772, straight stitches
Add a few stripes to lower and side petals

OUTLINE
All petals–1 strand 3774, backstitch or outline stitch

CENTRE
Throat–2 strands 972, straight stitches
Sides–2 strands 746, straight stitches or bullion stitches
Stigma–3 strands 472, French knot

THREADS	PETALS			THROAT & CENTRE		
DMC	3770	3772	3774	472	746	972
Finca	8140	7944	7933	4799	1211	1232
Appleton's	877	124	704	251A	871	555
Soie d'Alger	4241	4613*	2911	2123	crème	545

For Pennie Tyrrell

89. Lemon, Yellow & Gold Pansy Masterpiece

THREADS

DMC 743, 744, 3772, 3823,
(472, 746, 972)

Work petals for pansy with long and short stitch leaving the centre triangle and space for throat free of stitches.

LOWER PETAL

Outer row–3 strands 744
Inner rows–3 strands 743

SIDE PETALS

Outer row–3 strands 3823
Inner rows–3 strands 744

UPPER PETALS

All rows–3 strands 3823

STRIPES

Lower and side petals–1 strand 3772, straight stitches
Add a few stripes to lower and side petals

OUTLINE

Lower petal–1 strand 744, backstitch or outline stitch

Side and upper petals–1 strand 3823, backstitch or outline stitch

CENTRE

Throat–2 strands 972, straight stitches

Sides–2 strands 746, straight stitches or bullion stitches

Stigma–3 strands 472, French knot

THREADS	PETALS				THROAT & CENTRE		
DMC	743	744	3772	3823	472	746	972
Finca	1062	1137	7944	1128	4799	1211	1232
Appleton's	473	472	124	872	251A	871	555
Soie d'Alger	522	542	4613*	531	2123	crème	545

For Rosemary Cutter

90. Lemon & Yellow Pansy 'Masterpiece'

THREADS
DMC 307, 3078, 3772, (472, 746, 972)
Work petals for pansy with long and short stitch leaving the centre triangle and space for throat free of stitches.

LOWER PETAL
Outer row–3 strands 3078
Inner rows–3 strands 307

UPPER AND SIDE PETALS
All rows–3 strands 3078

STRIPES
Lower and side petals–1 strand 3772, straight stitches

Add a few stripes to lower petal and some shorter ones to the side petals.

OUTLINE
All petals–1 strand 3078, backstitch or outline stitch

CENTRE
Throat–2 strands 972, straight stitches

This pansy has quite a pronounced throat so make the stitches longer than usual

Sides–2 strands 746, straight stitches or bullion stitches

Stigma–3 strands 472, French knot

THREADS	PETALS			THROAT & CENTRE		
DMC	307	3078	3772	472	746	972
Finca	1222	1214	7944	4799	1211	1232
Appleton's	552*	841	124	251A	871	555
Soie d'Alger	535*	2121	4613*	2123	crème	545

For Colleen Lees

Heartsease *Viola tricolor*

Yet mark'd I where the bolt of
*   Cupid fell:*
It fell upon a little western flower,
Before milk-white, now purple with
*   love's wound,*
And maidens call it Love-in-idleness

Shakespeare
A Midsummer Night's Dream

Viola tricolor is the little flower Shakespeare writes of in *A Midsummer Night's Dream*.
It is the flower that caused Queen Titania to become 'enamoured of an ass'.

Many quaint names have been given to *Viola tricolor* in the past such as: Heartsease, Johnny Jump-up, Three faces under a hood, Tickle my fancy and Shakespeare's name for it Love-in-idleness. Today's pansies have been cultivated from this little flower.

If you have heartsease growing in your garden you will notice how their colours and markings vary, even on the same plant. Modern hybrids produce even more variations. As flowers mature they develop subtle shadings, and the markings on petals become more pronounced.

Heartsease are stitched in the same manner as pansies with long and short satin stitch. Whatever the size, heartsease require just two rows of stitching for a petal—an outer row and an inner row. The centre is also worked in the same way as for a pansy. Please read the chapter *How to Stitch a Pansy* before you begin. Follow the step-by-step embroidered samples and refer to the notes for the exact details.

You may prefer not to add an outline to your embroidered heartsease. They actually look quite good without and not adding it certainly cuts down on working time.

As well as the embroidered samples included in this chapter are drawings of heartsease in three different sizes and a conversion chart for the different threads.

Thread suggestions for working the different sized heartsease:

1. Small heartsease —2 strands DMC or Finca, or 1 strand Soie d'Alger

2. Medium heartsease —3 strands DMC or Finca, or 2 strands Soie d'Alger

3. Big heartsease—1 strand Appleton's

Try different thread combinations working with the threads listed or try matching and blending others as well. It's fun to experiment.

Some suggestions for other coloured threads you might like to try are:

DMC: 208, 307, 727, 3041, 3834, 3837

Finca: 2615, 1222, 1134, 1214, 8620, 2635*, 2627

Appleton's: 101, 102, 105, 356, 552, 554

Soie d'Alger: 521, 542, 1342, 2125, 2126, 3333, 3336, 5113, 5114, 5115, 5116

In the *Pansy Projects* chapter there are several projects and a couple of designs to give you ideas for stitching your own Heartsease.

For information on how to transfer a design, refer to MAKING TEMPLATES and TRANSFERRING DESIGNS, in the *Working Notes for Pansies* chapter.

The following specific instructions for heartsease are just to get you started. These instructions are for the medium sized heartsease (2) and the samples are stitched with DMC threads as listed. Work other sizes in the same manner with the appropriate thread, adjusting the stitch length and spacing of stitches.

You may want to add some buds and leaves to your heartsease. Work them in the same manner as for the pansies. Refer to BUDS, STEMS and LEAVES in the chapter *How to Stitch a Pansy*.

BUDS

1 or 2 strands of 155 or 208, satin stitch

Add a couple of stitches to the bud with 746 or 3823 if you like. New buds could be worked with just green (471) as for the calyx.

STEMS AND CALYXES

1 or 2 strands 471, stem stitch

LEAVES

2 or 3 strands 3346, satin stitch

Veins—1 strand 471, couching

Outline—1 strand 3346, backstitch

ROOTS

1 strand 739, backstitch

See drawings of Heartsease and leaves in three different sizes in the *Appendices*.

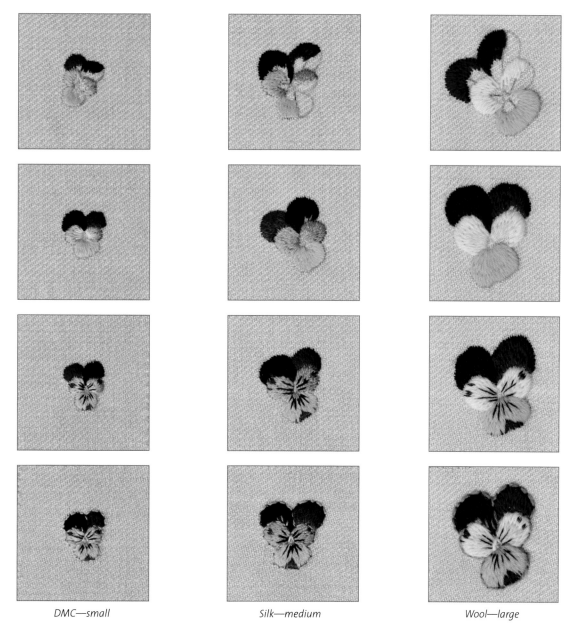

DMC—small   *Silk—medium*   *Wool—large*

Step-by-step Heartsease

1. Dark Mauve Heartsease

THREADS

DMC 155, 209, 327, 333, 550, 3371,
(472, 746, 972)

Work petals for heartsease with long
and short satin stitch leaving the
centre triangle and space for throat
free of stitches.

LOWER PETAL

Outer and inner rows–3 strands 444

'V' shaped mark: 3 strands 550,
straight stitch

Add purple mark to petal with four or
five small stitches adding the odd tiny
stitch slightly away from the others

SIDE PETAL

Outer and inner rows–blend 2 strands
209 and 1 strand 155

Spots (optional)–2 strands 327,
straight stitch

Add a small spot or two to side petals
if desired

For Victoria Reid

TOP PETALS

Outer and inner rows–3 strands 550

Stripes–1 strand 209, straight stitches

Add a paler touch to base of petals
with a few stitches

STRIPES

Lower and side petals–1 strand 3371,
straight stitches

Add 6 or 7 stripes to lower petal and
3 or 4 shorter ones to side petals

OUTLINE

All petals–1 strand 209, backstitch
or outline stitch

CENTRE

Throat–2 strands 972, straight stitches

Sides–1 strand 746, 3 straight stitches,
twice; or 2 bullions (7 wraps)

Stigma–2 strands 472, French knot

2. Light Mauve Heartsease

THREADS

DMC 210, 327, 340, 444, 550, 3042, 3371, (472, 746, 972)

Work petals for heartsease with long and short satin stitch leaving the centre triangle and space for throat free of stitches.

LOWER PETAL

Outer and inner rows: 3 strands 444

'V' shaped mark–3 strands 550, straight stitch

Add purple mark to petal with four or five small stitches adding the odd tiny stitch slightly away from the others

Shading (optional)–1 strand 3042, straight stitch

Add straight stitches to the edge of petal for a mauve touch

SIDE PETALS

Outer and inner rows–blend 2 strands 210 and 1 of 340

Spots (optional)–2 strands 327, straight stitch

Add a small spot or two to side petals if desired

For Christina Worth

TOP PETALS

Outer and inner rows–3 strands 550

Stripes–1 strand 3042, straight stitches

Add a paler touch to base of petals with a few stitches

STRIPES

Lower and side petals–1 strand 3371, straight stitches

Add 6 or 7 stripes to lower petal and 3 or 4 shorter ones to side petals

OUTLINE

All petals–1 strand 210, backstitch or outline stitch

CENTRE

Throat–2 strands 972, straight stitches

Sides–1 strand 746, 3 straight stitches, twice; or 2 bullions (7 wraps)

Stigma–2 strands 472, French knot

3. Lemon Heartsease

THREADS

DMC 327, 445, 550, 973, 3042, 3371, 3823, (472, 746, 972)

Work petals for heartsease with long and short satin stitch leaving the centre triangle and space for throat free of stitches.

LOWER PETAL

Outer and inner rows: 3 strands 973

'V' shaped mark–3 strands 550, straight stitch

Add purple mark to petal with four or five small stitches adding the odd tiny stitch slightly away from the others

SIDE PETALS

Outer row–3 strands 3823

Inner row–3 strands 445

Spots (optional)–2 strands 327, straight stitch

Add a small spot or two to side petals if desired

Shading (optional)–1 strand 3042, straight stitch

Add straight stitches to the edge of some petals for a mauve touch

For Sue Stanton

TOP PETALS

Outer and inner rows–3 strands 550

Stripes–1 strand 3042, straight stitches

Add a paler touch to base of petals with a few stitches

STRIPES

Lower and side petals–1 strand 3371, straight stitches

Add 6 or 7 stripes to lower petal and 3 or 4 shorter ones to side petals

OUTLINE

All petals–1 strand 3042, backstitch or outline stitch

CENTRE

Throat–2 strands 972, straight stitches

Sides–1 strand 746, 3 straight stitches or 2 bullions (7 wraps)

Stigma–2 strands 472, French knot

4. Light Mauve & Lemon Heartsease

THREADS

DMC 210, 327, 340, 445, 550, 973, 3371, (472, 746, 972)

Work petals for heartsease with long and short satin stitch leaving the centre triangle and space for throat free of stitches.

LOWER PETAL

Outer and inner rows–3 strands 973

'V' shaped mark–3 strands 550, straight stitch

Add purple mark to petal with four or five small stitches adding the odd tiny stitch slightly away from the others

SIDE PETALS

Outer row–blend 2 strands 210 and 1 of 340

Inner row–3 strands 445

Spots (optional)–2 strands 327, straight stitch

Add a small spot or two to side petals if desired

For Kerrie Blain

TOP PETALS

Outer and inner rows–3 strands 550

Stripes–1 strand 210, straight stitches

Add a paler touch to base of petals with a few stitches

STRIPES

Lower and side petals–1 strand 3371, straight stitches

Add 6 or 7 stripes to lower petal and 3 or 4 shorter ones to side petals

OUTLINE

All petals–1 strand 210, backstitch or outline stitch

CENTRE

Throat–2 strands 972, straight stitches

Sides–1 strand 746, 3 straight stitches, twice; or 2 bullions (7 wraps)

Stigma–2 strands 472, French knot

Thread Conversion Chart for Heartsease

DMC SIX STRAND FLOSS		FINCA	APPLETON'S WOOL	SOIE D'ALGER
155	medium dark blue violet	2699	894	1343
209	dark lavender	2606	451	3313
210	medium lavender	2606	885	3334*
327	dark, dark violet	—	455	3315
340	medium blue violet	2699*	893	1343
444	dark lemon	1227	553	536, 543
445	light lemon	1217	551	2523
471	very light avocado green	4885	543, 354	2124
472	ultra light avocado green	4799	251A	2122, 2123
550	very dark violet	2635*	456	3316
739	ultra very light tan	4000	851	05
746	off white	1211	871	crème
972	deep canary	1232	555	545
973	bright canary	1227	553	534
3042	light antique violet	8605	603	5112
3346	hunter green	4561	545, 546	2115
3371	black brown	8083	587	4146
3823	ultra pale yellow	1128	872	531

Pansy Projects

The projects on the following pages have been
worked by the The Pansy Group

(left to right)

Marion Trezise

Dianne Smith

Pam Arnott

Judy Spence

Lois Kinsman

Cheryl Armstrong

Diana Lampe

Maggie Taylor

Tiina Johnston

Allyson Hamilton

Jenny Brennan

Jan Jolliffe

Rita Crawford *(Absent)*

A PANSY SAMPLER

Pansies worked into a sampler make an attractive project to either frame or make into a cushion. It is also a good way to try out some different pansies.

All the pansies in this book are stitched into samplers. They were worked into three large samplers with 20 pansies each, two with nine pansies; one with four pansies and the others were all stitched singly. I think that a sampler of 12 pansies would also look good.

A sampler could be made up of a particular type or colour of pansy, like my blue pansy sampler or one of the 'Heirloom' or 'Masterpiece' pansies. It also looks great to have pansies of different colours, as they are in my large samplers.

An individual pansy in a frame makes a very special gift for a friend. A sampler of four pansies is an achievable project too, and looks lovely when framed. Four pansies would also be suitable for the front of a needle case.

My samplers are worked on linen twill and the pansies are stitched with DMC stranded cotton, as listed in the book.

When planning a sampler to be framed, allow plenty of linen around the sides. Measure 12 cm to 15 cm (4½" to 6") out from the grid on all sides.

Grid Lines

The grid for the sampler is divided into 6 cm (2 1/3") squares. Some people find preparing a grid a little confusing, so plan it carefully before pulling any threads out of the linen. You will pull the middle thread for an even number of pansies, but not for an odd number. Working from the middle, measure out the grid on the edge of your linen across the top and on one side. Mark with light pencil strokes and then pull out a thread of the linen for each grid line. These lines can be stitched over later with a running or stem stitch using a complementary coloured thread. I used two strands of DMC 3782 and I think it finishes the sampler off well.

Sampler of Nine Pansies

For a sampler of nine pansies you will need a piece of linen twill, approximately 42 cm (16 1/2") square and it should be washed before you start. Prepare the linen with a grid of nine 6 cm (2 1/3") squares as already explained, then choose and stitch the pansies. I used DMC stranded cotton for the pansies, as listed in the book. To finish off the sampler work through the grid lines with a neat running stitch.

Finished size of sampler in frame 30 cm (12") square

Marion Trezise's Sampler Cushion

Marion's lovely cushion of 16 woollen pansies is worked on a grid of 10 cm (4") squares. I think 9 cm (3 1/2") squares for the grid would work equally well with the benefit of framing the sampler with a 2 cm (3/4") border and making the pansies sit higher up on the cushion.

To make this cushion you will need a piece of linen twill, approximately 44 cm (17 1/2") square and it should be washed before you start. Prepare the linen with the grid as already explained, then choose and stitch the pansies. Marion has used Appleton's crewel wool, two threads for the pansies and one for the details. Work the lines for the grid in chain stitch with one thread of Appleton's 984.

Finished cushion size: 40 cm (16") square

A CIRCLE OF PANSIES

Pansies arranged in a circle make a very pleasing design for embroidery. A design suitable for many different projects such as the beautiful ones here made by Allyson, Judy and Dianne. They were all developed in the same way; even though sizes and materials are different the basic techniques are the same.

It really is fun to develop a design as you work, but you may find it easier to draw your design on paper before you start. If so refer to WORKING OUT YOUR OWN DESIGNS and TRANSFERRING DESIGNS. Begin by drawing the circles on paper and drawing the design over them. Read through the rest of this section for other information about working a circle of pansies.

Design as you Work

First of all mark your fabric with an outer circle and an inner circle, taking

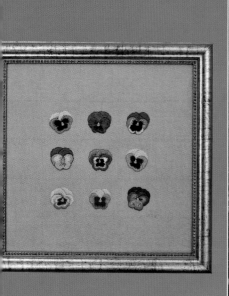

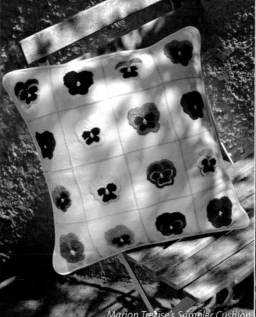

Diana Lampe's Sampler of Nine Pansies

Marion Trezise's Sampler Cushion

Judy Spence's Cushion

care to centre it. Run a thread around the circles as a lasting guide. These circles could become a feature of your design later on, worked in stem or chain stitch. See Dianne's blanket and also Marion's square cushion as examples.

Use templates for the pansies and draw around them, building up the design as you work. Stitch a pansy then draw another one. Place the pansies around the circle so that some overlap, tilt them at different angles and face them in different directions. The side-view of a pansy looks effective. When you have finished working the pansies you can add the buds and leaves. Just draw them straight onto the project or draw around templates if you find that easier. I like to have lots of greenery in a floral design and so often encourage people to add more leaves!

Working this way is exciting, choosing which pansy to do next and making it all work and come together... add an extra leaf here or a bud there.

Balance the Colours

Divide the circle roughly into three sections; this can be just in your mind. Use these sections to help you achieve balance when choosing the colours of pansies for your design. You need to consider particularly the bright, light or dark pansies, i.e. the ones that stand out the most. Have three or more areas of a bright colour like yellow, placing at least one in each section. This could be just a bud or petal. Positioning the bright colours this way will give life to your design and you'll find your eyes will be drawn around the circle.

To complete your design, embroider a circle or circles between the pansies with stem or chain stitch if you wish.

Judy Spence's Cushion

Judy's lovely cushion is worked on linen twill with two threads and one thread of Appleton's crewel wool. Finer details of the design are stitched with one thread, such as outlines, stripes and leaf veins. The design was developed as she worked as described above. She has chosen to use a mixed palette of colours for the pansies.

Finished cushion size: 40 cm (16") square

Circle sizes: 25 cm (10") across for outer and 19 cm (7 1/2") for inner

Allyson Hamilton's Picture

This gorgeous embroidery of Allyson's has an old-world charm about it. The frame really adds to this feeling and complements it well. The embroidery is worked on linen twill with DMC stranded cotton.

Allyson Hamilton's Picture

Dianne Smith's Blanket

Marion Trezise's Square of Pansies Cu...

Allyson has chosen to use 17 very different pansies and they do look lovely together. Her orange pansy No 60 adds warmth to the design. Allyson has been generous with the number of buds and leaves she's added to complete the embroidery.

Finished size in frame 30 cm (11 3/4") square

Circle sizes: 23.5 cm (9") across for outer and 17 cm (6 3/4") for inner

Dianne Smith's Blanket

Dianne has chosen blue, purple and yellow pansies with a touch of brown and cream for her blanket. She has used one thread of Appleton's crewel wool throughout. I'm sure you'll agree the effect is stunning! The design was developed as the pansies were stitched, as described before.

A fabric-marking pen was used to draw the pansies, heartsease and leaves onto the blanket. Dianne has enlarged the biggest of the heartsease in the *Appendices* even further for the blanket.

The circle of pansies has two rows of stem stitch added for the outer circle and just one for the inner. These are stitched with the same light green thread as used for the pansy stigma (Appleton's 251A). Although the embroidered circles are subtle I think they really bring the design together.

Dianne has backed the blanket with a cotton/wool mix cream fabric and bound it with a violet blue cotton fabric. On the back she has worked her own pansy No 82 as well as a heartsease, her name, and the year.

Finished blanket size: 100 cm (39 1/2") square

Circle size: 43 cm (17") across for outer and 35 cm (14") for inner

A SQUARE OF PANSIES

Marion Trezise's Square of Pansies Cushion

Although the design for Marion's beautiful cushion is square, it is worked in the same way as a circle of pansies. A rough drawing of the design was made before she started working. Just follow the previous instructions building up the design over two squares rather than two circles. Marion has worked on linen twill and used Appleton's crewel wool, two threads for the pansies and one for the details.

The finished design has the outer square worked in chain stitch, just peeping through between the pansies. The square and lattice are stitched with a thread to match the linen twill (Appleton's 984). The lines for the lattice are also worked in chain stitch and are 3.2 cm (1 1/4") apart. I think the understated embroidery of the

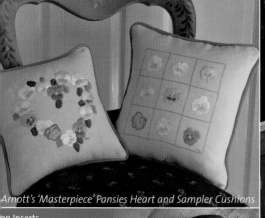

on Inserts

putting a lot of time into
ng a cushion you might
think about using a
er and down insert.
give your cushion a
soft look as well as
g quite luxurious.

Pam Arnott's Silk Evening Purse

Tiina Johnston's Cushions

square and lattice just finish the cushion off perfectly.

Finished cushion size: 40 cm (16") square

Square sizes: 30 cm (11 3/4 ") across for outer and 23 cm (9") for inner

A HEART OF PANSIES

Pam Arnott's Heart of Pansies

I designed this heart of pansies especially for the 'Masterpiece' pansies. Pam Arnott has stitched the design with these lovely pansies and made it into a small cushion.

I think this design would look beautiful with the pansies worked in soft pink through to dark red, perhaps on silk and using silk threads. It would make a very romantic gift either framed or made into a cushion. I have added a few extra leaves to the design to be found in the *Appendices*. Refer to TRANSFERRING DESIGNS for advice on how to transfer the design.

Pam's finished cushion size: 26 cm (10 1/4 ")

AN EVENING PURSE

Pam Arnott's Silk Evening Purse

The pansies on this lovely black silk purse of Pam's are embroidered with Soie d'Alger silk threads. It is a very special accessory to take out in the evening with you.

TWO LOVELY CUSHIONS

Tiina Johnston's Cushions

The inspiration for Tiina's beautiful cushions was a faded and worn but nevertheless much loved cushion. Her Grandmother Elsa, in Finland, made it 40 years ago. Elsa's interest in needlework and weaving was a great influence on Tiina as she grew up.

Tiina has cleverly adapted the design using pansies from this book. She worked the cushions in mirror image on linen twill with DMC stranded

cotton. The design is reproduced for you in the *Appendices*. Enlarge it on a photocopier to the size you want. I think the design also lends itself to being worked in Appleton's crewel wool.

Finished cushion size: 43 cm (17")

Design size: 25 cm (10") by 23 cm (9")

PICTURES OF PANSIES

'Pansies'

You'll enjoy embroidering this picture of pansies and the pleasure will continue when it's hanging on your wall. Your spirits will be lifted each time you catch a glimpse of the faces of the pansies.

I have given the particular pansies used for my embroidery, but the design can of course be worked with any combination of pansies you like. I think blues and yellows would look very stylish.

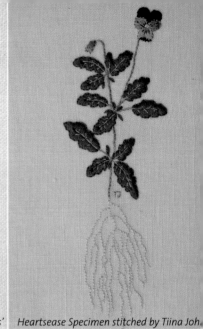

Diana Lampe's 'Pansies'   *Heartsease Specimen stitched by Tiina Joh.*

My picture has been worked on embroidery linen with DMC stranded cotton. You will find the design reproduced for you in actual size in the *Appendices*. The pansy numbers appear on the design. Refer to TRANSFERRING DESIGNS for advice on how to transfer the design to your fabric.

You might like to try another combination of pansies that worked well for an earlier design. Place the following pansies clockwise: Nos 2, 54, 71, 18, 44, 31, and 16. Add buds with threads used for these pansies to balance the design.

Size in frame 23 cm (9") x 17.5 cm (7")

Heartsease Specimen
I drew this little plant after carefully removing the soil from the roots. Tiina Johnston has worked it with one strand of DMC. I think it would also be beautiful worked with one strand of silk. You will find the drawing in actual size in the *Appendices*. Refer to Transferring Designs for advice on how to do this and read through the instructions in the *Heartsease* chapter for details on the threads and stitches to use.

Jenny Brennan's Carpet of Muted Pansies
This lovely picture of Jenny's is similar in style to the embroidery of mine on the cover of this book. Jenny has chosen 'Heirloom' pansies and other muted pansies for the project and has added quite a few leaves between. Her picture is worked on linen twill with DMC stranded cotton.

You too can design and stitch a project like this. Refer to WORKING OUT YOUR OWN DESIGNS, BALANCE THE COLOURS, and TRANSFERRING DESIGNS.
I have planned for a long time to work a carpet of pansies in wool for a cushion. Perhaps you might be inspired to do this too.

Finished embroidery size: 15 cm (6") x 14 cm (5 1/2")
Size inside frame:
25 cm (10") x 23.5 cm (9 1/2")

Maggie Taylor's Sampler of Pansies
This embroidery of Maggie's started life as a sampler of 20 pansies! She has added extra pansies making 39 in all with stems and leaves. The overall effect is both delicate and airy.

Finished size of embroidery in frame: 36 cm (14") x 28 cm (11")

Jenny Brennan's Heartsease Pictures
These delightful little pictures are worked on linen twill with DMC stranded cotton. For some ideas on working these or similar heartsease designs refer to the embroidery notes for the spectacle case and read through WORKING OUT YOUR OWN DESIGNS, BALANCE THE COLOURS, and TRANSFERRING DESIGNS.

Jenny Brennan's Heartsease Heart

tail from Jenny Brennan's Carpet of Muted Pansies

Detail from Maggie Taylor's Sampler of Pansies

Jenny Brennan's Carpet of Heartsease

Carpet of Heartsease

Draw the design on paper first for the 'carpet' of heartsease and then transfer it to your fabric. Embroider the heartsease and leaves with various DMC stranded cottons chosen from those suggested in the instructions.

Finished embroidery size:
7 cm (2 3/4") square.

Heartsease Heart

Jenny reduced the 'heart of pansies' design right down for this little heart and added some extra leaves. You will see that she has been quite imaginative with her heartsease.

Finished embroidery size: 9 cm (3 1/2") x 9 cm (3 1/2")

Marion Trezise's Rust Pansies

This project is made up of 10 pansies, including one viewed from the side and a bud. I think they appear to be hanging in the air. All the pansies chosen by Marion are in rust shades, some with yellow. Marion has added stems to the pansies. The finished embroidery is surrounded with a circular mount that shows the design off well.

Circle in mat: 17.5 cm (7")

Size inside frame 26.5 cm
(10 1/2") square

Marion Trezise's Rust Pansies

Four Small Projects

I think it's a good idea to make something small and special just for you, a personal item to use and enjoy. It will give pleasure whenever you use it and I'm sure be much admired by others.

A NEEDLE CASE

Finished needle case is approximately 13 cm (5") square. Pattern for needlecase in *Appendices* at end of book.

Requirements

30 x 28 cm (12" x 11") embroidery linen or fabric of your choice, washed

Needles, threads and hoop for embroidery

2 skeins DMC stranded cotton for cord and tassels

Tapestry needle and crewel No 7 needle

Embroidery thread winder (optional)

2 pieces Doctor's flannel 12 x 24 cm (4 3/4" x 9 1/2")

Pinking shears

Pearl button or other button for closing

Marion Trezise's needle case is stitched with several heartsease and leaves and Tiina Johnston's with four 'Heirloom' pansies. The pansies are worked in a grid of 5.5 cm (2 1/8") squares. The grid is centred giving a 1 cm border. Tiina hasn't stitched the lines of the grid on her needle case, but you can if you like.

You can make a needle case any size you wish but take care when positioning your design on the front. This is a little tricky because the seam allowance is only on three sides.

Preparation

Make a paper pattern for the needle case by photocopying or tracing the pattern from the *Appendices*. Place the spine on a folded piece of paper, then cut out and open up. If you copy the pattern to the top of a page you can just fold it over at the spine and cut out.

Place the needle case pattern on the fold of fabric and cut out. Don't cut through the fold along the bottom just yet, as it's easier to embroider on a bigger piece of fabric.

Mark the centre of the front of needle case with a mark or tailor's tack. Mark the 1 cm seam allowance and the spine too, if you wish. Fold linen in half again along the spine, forming your needle case.

Transfer the design to the front of the needle case making sure it is centred. See TRANSFERRING DESIGNS for details.

Embroidery

Embroider your design on the front of the needle case and add a small detail to the back if you wish.

Making up

Tidy up the back of your work making sure there are no tags, which could show through when you make up the needle case.

Hand wash (but not if using silk threads) and press your finished piece carefully. See WASHING AND PRESSING for more information.

Cut through the fold, place right sides together and pin. Machine stitch the needle case seams together, leaving an opening for turning through. Trim corners, turn through and sew up the opening by hand. Tack along the seam to give a crisp edge. Press well and then remove tacking.

Using a pair of pinking shears cut two pieces of doctor's flannel a little smaller than the needle case. Place these inside the needle case and either pin or stitch into position.

Now make a tassel and the cord. The other tassel will be made later.

Tassels

1. Cut out a 5 cm (2") square piece of card to use for winding the tassel. Make a little cut near one corner to hold the thread ends.

2. Wrap DMC stranded cotton around the card 25 times. Slip the beginning and ending threads into the cut at the bottom of the card.

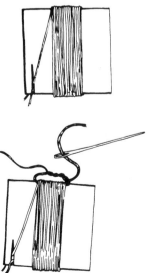

3. Take a length of thread and thread onto a tapestry needle. Thread under the threads at the top of card and tie the loops together securely. Twist the thread twice to stop it slipping when tying the knot. This is the tying thread.

4. Slip the tied loops off the card, freeing the ends at the same time.

5. Take another length of thread and tie it around the loops towards the top, wind several times and secure. Thread the ends onto a tapestry needle and take them down through the centre of the tassel.

6. Cut the loops through at the lower edge and trim neatly.

Cord

7. Cut three lengths of DMC stranded cotton 125 cm (49 1/2") long. Knot together at one end and pin to an ironing board or tie to a door handle.

8. Thread the tassel onto the length of threads and position halfway along.

9. Holding the thread taut at the unattached end, twist either by hand or with a thread-winder until the threads start to kink.

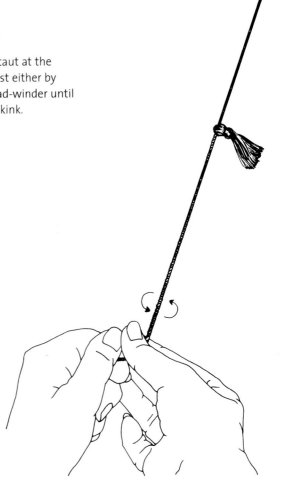

10. Take hold of the twisted threads in the centre, where the tassel is positioned and let go of the end. Allow it to twist together forming a cord. You may need to adjust the twists along the cord to make them even.

11. Remove the cord from the ironing board or door handle.

12. Bind the ends of cord together to prevent it unravelling and stitch through a couple of times to make really secure. Trim ends.

Making and Attaching the Second Tassel

13. To make and attach the second tassel, pull the twists in the cord apart at the end and actually make the tassel through the opening. Position the cord's join inside the tassel head and then adjust the twists along the cord again to finish.

Attaching the Cord

Wrap the cord around the needle case and tie into position. Work two small buttonhole shanks as hinges on the outside of the spine over the cord, holding it in place. At the same time stitch over the cord inside. This will hold the flannel in place as well.

Closing

On the back of the needle case, sew the button halfway down the edge. Using three or four strands of matching thread, make a buttonhole loop in the same position on the front. Be sure the button fits through the loop.

This method for making cord requires threads to be cut two and a half times longer than the finished cord length.

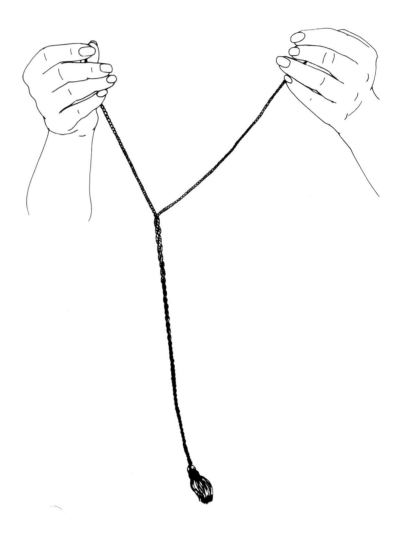

A PUMPKIN-SHAPED PINCUSHION

Finished pincushion is approximately 13 cm (5") across.

Requirements

20 cm square embroidery linen or other fabric, washed

Fabric for underside of pincushion, washed

Needles, threads and hoop for embroidery

DMC stranded cotton or other thread, for tying

Darning needle

2 buttons

Needle grabber (optional)

Preparation

Decide on the finished size pincushion you want to make and allow 1 cm for seam all around. With a round template such as a plate or with a compass, draw circles on your fabric, the inner circle for stitching and the outer one for cutting.

Don't cut out the circle just yet as it's easier to embroider on a bigger piece of fabric. This will also prevent the edge stretching and fraying. Fold linen into halves, quarters and eighths. Run a tacking thread along these fold lines to mark the segments, as well as around the circles.

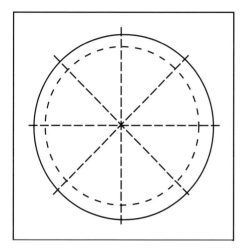

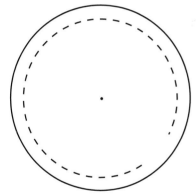

Embroidery

Work embroidery on every segment, every second one or just five on one side of pincushion. This is to leave space for the pins! The embroidery should be positioned to sit high on the finished pincushion so don't stitch too close to the edge or the centre.

Large Pumpkin-shaped Pincushion by Dianne Smith; small ones by Jenny Brennan; square pincushion by Marion Trezise

Making Up

Tidy up the back of your work making sure there are no tags, which could show through when you make up the pincushion. Remove the tacking threads except for the cutting line. Mark the centre front with a tailor's tack.

Hand wash (but not if using silk threads) and press your finished piece carefully. See WASHING AND PRESSING for more information.

Cut top of pincushion out, around the cutting line. Cut another piece of fabric the same size for the underside. This could be the fabric used for the front, a Liberty lawn, a floral or plain green fabric. Mark the centre back with a tailor's tack.

With right sides facing pin together and stitch by machine, leaving a small opening to turn pincushion through. Turn it through and then fill firmly with Dacron, lamb's wool or other filling. Sew the opening up by hand.

Add a decorative stitch such as Palestrina stitch around the seam if you like.

Thread darning needle with 3 metres ($3^1/_4$ yards) of three strands of thread. Double the thread over and knot the ends together. Stitch down through the centre of the pincushion, losing the knot inside. Wrap threads around pincushion and stitch down through the centre first into halves, then quarters and finally eighths. Pull firmly each time forming a pumpkin shape. A needle grabber will make it easier to pull the needle through.

Add buttons to the centre of pincushion, one on the top and another on the underside. Finish the thread off securely, losing the end inside the pincushion.

SPECTACLE CASE

The design is reproduced for you in the *Appendices* in actual size.

Requirements

20 cm (8") square linen twill or fabric of your choice, washed

20 cm (8") square fabric for lining such as stretch velveteen or flannelette

Embroidery transfer pencil and tracing paper

Needles, threads and hoop for embroidery

The heartsease spectacle case is worked on linen twill with one thread of Appleton's crewel wool.

Marion Trezise's spectacle case is also worked on linen twill and has three pansies stitched with Appleton's crewel wool (2 threads and 1 thread). She has chosen three of the deep pink pansies Nos 68, 69 and 71 to use and has also added a bud and two leaves to the back. The edge is worked with

Palestrina stitch in Appleton's 984. Marion used an interfacing of iron-on pellon to give more body to her spectacle case.

Preparation

Make a paper pattern for the spectacle case by photocopying or tracing the pattern. Transfer the design onto the linen. See TRANSFERRING DESIGNS for details.

Don't cut out the spectacle case just yet, as it's easier to embroider on a larger piece of fabric. The transferred design tends to wear off the linen as you work so baste the outline for a more lasting guide. You may like to mark the seam line in this way as well.

Embroidery

Embroider the heartsease design and leaves with one thread of various Appleton's crewel wools. Choose the threads from those suggested in the instructions. It's fun deciding whether to stitch a paler or brighter heartsease.

Don't worry it's easy once you start and you really can't go wrong with these delightful little flowers. Add the stripes to the heartsease with one strand DMC stranded cotton 3371.

Making up

Tidy up the back of your work making sure all ends are secure. Hand wash (but not if using silk threads) and press your finished piece carefully. See WASHING AND PRESSING for more information.

Cut out the spectacle case and lining in the same size. Place spectacle case and lining right sides together, pin and machine stitch the seams, leaving an opening for turning through. Trim corners, turn through and sew up the opening by hand. Tack along the seam to give a crisp edge then press well and remove tacking. Fold the spectacle case over and pin, then stitch across the lower edge and up the side with a neat hemstitch.

Finish the edge if you wish with a decorative stitch such as Palestrina stitch using a matching or contrasting thread.

A PANSY BROOCH

Requirements

Template plastic

20 cm x 12 cm (8" x 5") linen twill or fabric of your choice, washed

Small piece of pellon

8 cm (3") hoop

Needles and threads for embroidery

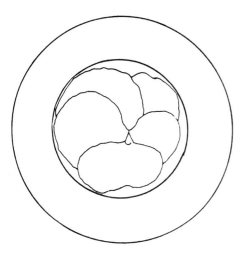

Pansy Brooches Diana Lampe (front) Jenny Bradford (behind)

Scissors for cutting plastic and fabric and threads

Sewing thread to match fabric

Brooch pin

It is a good idea to use plastic rather than cardboard for inside the brooch so it can easily be washed or dry-cleaned. If you don't have any template plastic, use a piece of plastic taken from the flat side of a large fruit juice bottle.

Preparation

Cut out two small circles in template plastic for the front and back of brooch. Trace them from the illustration or draw around the lid of a film case. Cut a circle of pellon in the same size to pad your brooch.

Make a plastic template of the larger circle or find a small glass the same size. This is for the cutting line. Cut a 12 cm (5") square from one end of the linen. Using the templates mark the two circles on the linen. Centre the

large circle first and then carefully position the smaller one inside. They need to be fairly even but you can judge this by eye. Don't cut out the circle of linen just yet.

Embroidery

Draw a pansy inside the smaller circle either freehand or using a pansy template. Now place in a hoop and embroider your chosen pansy.

Making Up

Wash and press your embroidered pansy (don't wash if using silk threads). Cut out the circle of linen and also another one for the back of the brooch.

Position carefully and sew the brooch pin to the circle of linen for the back, using a double thread of sewing cotton. If you like stitch through the plastic at the same time to make it really strong. Pierce holes in the plastic before you start.

With a double thread of sewing cotton run a gathering stitch around the edge of both circles of linen. Remember to put in the pellon padding for the pansy. Draw up the gathers over the small plastic circles. Adjust gathers for a firm and even finish and stitch to secure.

Join the front and back together around the edge with slipstitch. Finish off the edge with a simple cross-stitch (2 strands) or the more decorative Palestrina stitch using a matching or contrasting thread. I used four strands of DMC 3782 for the Palestrina stitch edge on my brooch, but DMC Coton Perlé 8 would also be a good choice.

Jenny Bradford has stitched her own pansy No 24 on her brooch and trimmed the edge with Mill Hill beads. The pink pansy brooch is also made by Jenny.

Crocheted Pansies

I was using an old and tattered pansy tea-cosy during a class several years ago and I mentioned that I'd love to have a tea-cosy made with more realistic pansies. Everyone thought this a great idea, but we needed a pattern. A skilled knitter and crocheter, Marion Trezise decided she could do it. We chose to use Appleton's crewel wool for the crocheted pansies so they could be worked in the same colours as the embroidered ones. What an exciting prospect!

This little seed of an idea germinated and grew into the following chapter showing how to crochet pansies and go on and make your own gorgeous tea-cosy, coffee-cosy or perhaps a posy of pansies for your lapel. Marion has spent much time on this project and has done a wonderful job developing the patterns, writing the instructions and working the samples.

Crocheted pansies are not unlike embroidered pansies in that they take a little practice. Marion can whip one up in no time, but if you are having any trouble ask an experienced crocheter to help you.

BASIC PANSY PATTERN

Materials Needed

Appletons Embroidery Wool is used to create the pansies in the colours as listed below.

Purple Pansy: Purple No 456 and Deep Purple No 106

Blue Pansy: Blue No 896 and Deep Purple No 106

Maroon Pansy: Maroon No 149 and Black No 993

Tan Pansy: Tan No 723 and Black No 993

Pink Pansy: Pink No 145 and Deep Pink No 716

Yellow Pansy: Yellow No 554 and Brown No 187

Centres of all the pansies are worked in Yellow No 554

Leaves: Dark Green No 546 and Lighter Green 545

Crochet Hooks Numbered 3.00, 2.50 and 2.00 mm

Note: The hook size is only a guide. You may use a size to give you the size pansy or leaf that you desire.

1 small safety pin for marking positions as instructed

1 large eye tapestry needle for darning in the ends

As a guide to the amount of wool required for pansies allow the following:

1 skein of outer petal colour will make 3 pansies

1 skein of inner petal colour will make 6 pansies

1 skein of green will make 7 large leaves

Therefore one skein of each pansy colour, plus two skeins of dark green and one of lighter green will make 18 pansies, 14 dark leaves and seven lighter ones.

To cover the tea-cosy entirely in pansies 24 pansies and 20 leaves will be required, or more if you prefer. The second cosy requires 10 pansies and 12 leaves. The smaller cosy has a posy of five pansies and three leaves.

BASIC PANSY

Base Ring

Using hook No 3.00 and yellow No 554 begin by making a base on which to create the pansy. Make a loop on the hook, secure and work a chain of four. Make the chain into a ring by working a sl st into the first ch.

This will be referred to throughout as the **base ring**.

Work * 3 ch, sl st into ring. * Repeat * to * 3 times.

Note: Make sure that the sl sts are worked into the centre ring NOT the centre of a ch st. A small safety pin may be used to mark the centre at the time of making the ring.

This process makes four small loops around part of the ring.

Work five dc around the remaining part of the ring. End off. The right side of the work is facing. Finish off ends carefully by securing with a small backstitch and then neatly and securely darning them into the back of the work.

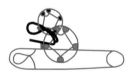

The base ring is now completed as illustrated and numbered for the petals 1–5.

Upper Petals (1 & 2)

Using the paler shade of the chosen coloured pansy, and beginning with a secured loop on the hook, and right side of work facing, join into loop 1 with a sl st, 1 ch.

Row 1: 5 dc into loop, 1 ch, turn

Row 2: (1 dc, 1 tr, 1 dtr), in first dc, 3 dtr in each of next 3 dc,
(1 dtr, 1 tr, 1dc) in next dc,
sl st into base loop, 1 ch, turn

Row 3: *1 dc, 1 ch* in first st. Repeat * to * 14 times around the edge of petal, 1 dc, into last st, sl st into base loop. This completes petal 1.

Do not end off. Start petal 2 with a sl st into loop 2, 1 ch. Repeat as for petal 1. End off.

Finish off ends carefully by neatly darning them into the back of the work.

Lower Petals (3, 4 & 5)

Using darker shade of chosen coloured pansy and beginning with a secured loop on the hook, and right side of work facing, join into loop 3 with a sl st, 1 ch. Mark the 1 ch with a small safety pin.

Petal 3: 1 dc, 5 tr, 1 dc, 1 ch into same loop.

Petal 4: Crossing over in front of petals 1 & 2, work sl st into loop 4, 1 ch, 1 dc, 5 tr, 1 dc into the same loop.

Petal 5: On the base ring, 1 dc into first dc,
1 dc, 1 tr, 5 dtr, 1 tr into second dc,
1 tr into third dc,
1 tr, 5 dtr, 1 tr, 1 dc into fourth dc,
1 dc into fifth dc,
Sl st into first st of petal 3 as marked with a safety pin.

DO NOT REMOVE PIN.
Finish off ends by neatly darning them into the back of the work.

Outer edge of pansy

Using paler shade of the chosen pansy colour, beginning with a secured loop on the hook, and right side of work facing, join into the beginning of petal 3 (as marked with the safety pin) with a sl st, 1 ch.

Petal 3: * 1 dc into first st, (same st as sl st),
1 dc, 1 tr into 2nd st,
2 tr into each of sts 3, 4 and 5,
1 tr, 1 dc into sixth st,
1 dc into seventh st *
Work st st under the 1 ch of previous row.

Petal 4: Join into beginning of petal 4 with a sl st, 1 ch.
repeat * to * as for petal 3.

The next st is a dc worked over the darker colour and into the yellow base ring. This stitch defines the separation between the petals 4 and 5.

Petal 5: *1 dc, 1 ch* into first st,
Repeat * to * 6 times around petal,
1 dc into next 3 sts, 1 ch,
Repeat * to * 6 times 1 dc.

The next stitch is a dc worked over the darker colour and into the yellow base ring. This stitch defines the separation between the petals 5 and 3.

Petal 3: # 1 dc into first and second sts,
*1 dc, 1 ch * into next st,
Repeat * to * 6 times,
1 dc into each of next 3 sts #,
Work sl st into last stitch.

Petal 4: Repeat # to # for Petal 4.

Finish the pansy with a sl st. End off. Neatly darn in ends as before.

Note: For a larger and more frilled lower petal, repeat the final instructions for petal 5 working the 1 dc into the 1 ch of the previous row, in addition to all or some of the 1 dc according to the frilled effect desired

CROCHETING THE EMBROIDERED PANSIES

Now that you have found out how easy it is to crochet delightful pansies, you may like to try some of the other pansies that are featured in this book.

With a few modifications to the basic pattern, any colour combination can be achieved. When more than two colours are introduced, ending off, and beginning with a new colour will be more frequent, and an extra row of 1 ch, 1 dc on petal No 5 will be necessary. The extra row will increase the size of the pansy slightly and add to the frilled affect. If only a slight frilled look is desired, work 1 ch between only every second 1 dc. In some designs with a blended effect, a blend of two strands of wool together can be used.

LEAF PATTERN

Note: The centre vein of the leaf is worked using wool doubled. All other stitches are worked into this vein using a single strand. Directions are given for longer sized leaves. Shorter leaves may be made by following instructions as indicated throughout the directions. To make leaves smaller still a smaller size hook may be used. Generally use darker wool for larger leaves and lighter for smaller ones.

Begin with a length of wool 80 cm (32"). Fold in half and use double. Using hook No 2.50 mm make a chain of 13 (less for a shorter leaf) which will

be the centre vein of the leaf. End off wool.

Row 1

Using wool single, secure a loop on the hook. Leaving 3 ch free for the stem begin with 1 dc into the fourth ch and proceed as follows :

1 dc into next st,

1 dc, 1 tr into next st,

2 tr into each of next 5 sts,
   (less if for shorter leaf)

1 tr into next st,

3 tr into next st (these sts form the pointed end of the leaf),

Work the return side of the leaf as follows :

1 tr into next st,

2 tr into each of next 5 sts
   (or number to equal first side),

1 tr, 1 dc into next st,

1 dc into next st,

1 dc into next st, 1 ch.

This is the right side of the leaf. Keeping leaf with right side facing, carry the ch behind the 3 ch stem and continue as follows:

Final row

Begin with 1 dc into each of first 3 sts, 2 ch,

Work * 1 dc into next 2 sts, 2 ch, *

Repeat * to * 5 times
   (less for shorter leaf),

Continue around the end of the leaf with 1 dc in next 2 sts, (1 dc, 2 ch, 1 dc) in next st, 1 dc in next 2 sts, 2 ch,

Repeat * to * 5 times (or number equal to repeats on first side),

End with 1 dc into each of last 3 sts. Sl st into centre of stem and end off. Darn in ends carefully to complete leaf.

For a variation of colour for the leaves green Nos 355 and 356 may be used.

KNITTED TEA-COSY IN RIB DESIGN

Requirements

2 x 50 gm balls of 8 ply wool

1 pair No 3.25 mm knitting needles
   No 3.50 mm crochet hook

Begin by casting on 53 sts.

Row 1: Sl1, K1, P2, (K2, P2)
   until last st, K1.

Repeat Row 1 until work measures between 13–15 cm (5"–6") long or as desired.

With right side facing shape top as follows:

Row 1: (K2 tog, P2) to last st,
   K1. (40 sts)

Row 2: Sl1, (K2, P1) to end of row.

Row 3: Sl1, (P1, K2 tog) to end of row.
   (27 sts)

Row 4: Sl1, (K1, P1) to end of row.

Row 5: Sl1, (K2 tog) to end of row.
   (14 sts)

Row 6: Sl1, purl to end of row.

Tea-Cosies by Marion Trezise and embroidered doiley by Allyson Hamilton

Row 7: Sl1, (wl fwd, K2 tog) to end of row, K1.

Row 8: Sl1, purl to end of row.

Row 9: Sl1, knit into front and back of each st to last st, K1. (26 sts)

Row 10: Sl1, (K1, P1) to last st, K1.

Row 11: As row 10.

Row 12: As row 11.

Cast off in rib.

Repeat for the other side of the cosy.

Darn all ends into the knitting with a tapestry needle and stitch up the side seams leaving openings on each side for the handle and spout of the teapot.

Using wool double and a No 3.50 mm crochet hook, crochet a length of cord in chain stitch approximately 50 cm (20") long. Darn in the ends. Thread the cord through the holes at the top of the cosy as tightly as desired according to the size teapot and tie firmly in a bow.

PANSY COVERED COSY

Place the cosy on the teapot. The cord around the top can be pulled in as tightly or loosely as desired depending on the size of the teapot and the desired effect. For the pansy covered cosy leave the frill at the top of the cosy standing up and arrange the pansies and leaves to cover most of the cosy. The number required will depend on the size of the teapot. Carefully stitch the pansies on to the cosy in the centre of each pansy and along the centre vein of each leaf. Some petals may be stitched with a single stitch if needed, but the aim is to leave the pansies as free and natural as possible.

COSY WITH PANSY BORDER

Place the cosy on the teapot. The cord around the top can be pulled in as tightly or loosely as desired depending on the size of the teapot and the desired effect. For the pansy bordered cosy leave the frill at the top of the cosy standing up and arrange five pansies and five leaves around each side of the lower edge of the cosy.

A leaf may also be added under the spout and handle making a total number of 10 pansies and 12 leaves. Carefully stitch the pansies on to the cosy in the centre of each pansy and along the centre vein of each leaf. Some petals may be stitched with a single stitch if needed, but the aim is to leave the pansies as free and natural as possible.

BUNCH-TOP COSY

This cosy is made with the cord tied on the inside of the cosy leaving a small hole and the frill is also turned to the inside. Make a bunch of pansies as for the instructions for the posy of pansies, either with or without calyx, and either large or small pansies, and pull the stems through the hole at the top of the cosy. Arrange as desired and turning the cosy inside out, carefully stitch the stems to the inside of the cosy.

COFFEE-COSY

Instead of a tea-cosy you may like a cosy to keep the coffee pot hot. The coffee-cosy in the photograph was knitted from the same pattern as the tea-cosy, using only 45 stitches and knitted to the measurements of the height of the pot before the shaping rows were worked. As the number of stitches required is divisible by four, plus one, any size cosy can be created to fit any size coffee pot.

POSY OF PANSIES
(with calyx)

Requirements

Five Pansies in colours as chosen from basic pattern using size 3.00 mm hook. Three leaves in chosen colour green.

Calyx

The calyx for each pansy is constructed by first crocheting five separate sepals.

Using green wool No 545 and No 2.00 mm hook begin with a secured loop on the hook and work seven chain. Work around the sepal as follows :

Leave first 2 ch, 1 dc into each of next 3 ch, sl st into remaining 2 ch, then work 3 ch at the end of sepal.

Return on the opposite side with sl st into next 2 ch, 1 dc into next 3 ch, and sl st into centre of sepal.

End off leaving approximately 60 cm (24") of wool for using to crochet the stem.

Darn in the small end.

Repeat this process four more times. (5 sepals)

Place all sepals together evenly and using a separate strand of green wool about 30 cm (12"), tie all sepals together firmly at the base. Leave the ends of the strand of wool for future use.

Stems

Using No 2.50 mm hook, and the five strands held together, crochet a stem from the sepals downwards. Begin with a loop on the hook and work in chain stitch to desired length. End off and darn each end separately into the end of the stem at varying lengths. Make a caylx for each pansy.

The finished stem is looped into a knot at the base of the sepals to give a firm finish. Using the loose tie ends from the stem, stitch a caylx to the back of each pansy.

Lightly steam each pansy and stem and gently pull into shape.

DO NOT PRESS

Stems for Leaves

Using green wool No 545 in treble thickness and with a No 2.50 mm hook make a chain approximately 9 cm (3 1/2") in length. End off and darn ends separately into the ends of the stem leaving one end loose. With the loose end stitch a stem to a leaf. Repeat for 2 more leaves.

To make posy

Holding the stems of the five pansies and the three leaves together tie firmly together using a double strand of green wool. Tie off securely. Gently manipulate the flowers and leaves until a pleasing arrangement is achieved.

PANSY BROOCH

(without calyx)

Requirements

5 Pansies in colours chosen from basic pattern using hook No 2.50 mm

3 leaves in green No 545 using hook No 2.00 mm

(These pansies and leaves will be smaller than the ones on the cosies)

1 small brooch clip

Small amount of black felt and soft wadding

Stems for pansies and leaves

Using green wool No 545 in treble thickness and with a No 2.50 mm hook make a chain approximately 9 cm (3½") in length. End off and darn ends seperately into the ends of the stem leaving one end loose. With the loose end stitch a leaf or pansy to the end of the stem. Repeat until all the pansies and leaves have a stem attached.

To make posy

Make posy as above.

Backing Piece

This is a small circular piece approximately 5 cm (2") in diameter, on to which the pansies are arranged and stitched. Cut two pieces of black felt 5 cm (2") in diameter and using buttonhole or stab stitch join the pieces together around the edge leaving a small opening. Pad lightly with wadding and then complete the stitching.

Assemble the posy of pansies on to the pad in a pleasing arrangement and stitch the centres of each pansy onto the pad. As the leaves are attached to stems it will not be necessary to stitch the leaves down.

Finish by stitching the brooch clip to the back of the pad making sure to keep it straight with the line of the posy.

© Marion Trezise 2005

Only a few knitted tea-cosies have been illustrated in this book. One features the blue and yellow pansies on a soft purple cosy. Another has pink and rust pansies on a moss green cosy. Which pansies would complement your teapot or teacups?

Rita Crawford's Tea-cosy

The Stitches

Pansies and most other embroidery should be worked in a hoop and stitched with a stabbing motion i.e. one stitch down and the next one up. To make it easier for you to understand how a stitch works, these diagrams actually show the needle scooping onto the next place it will emerge, rather than stabbing.

There are exceptions to this general rule and you'll find it is easier to work bullion stitch and lazy daisy bullion stitch with the embroidery removed from the hoop.

Left-handed embroiderers can reverse the stitch diagrams by looking at them in a mirror

Embroidery Stitches

Long and Short Stitch

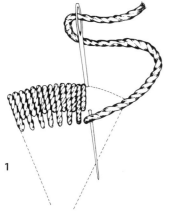

1

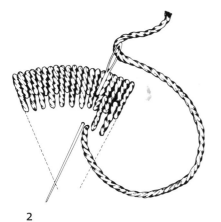

2

Straight Stitch

Satin Stitch—slanted

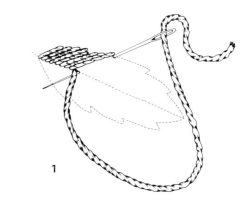

1

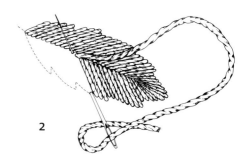

2

Stem Stitch

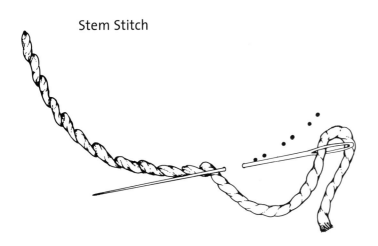

Backstitch

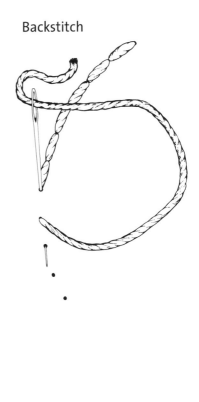

Outline Stitch

Couching

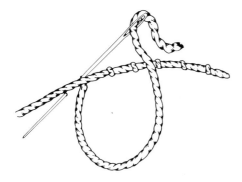

Lazy Daisy Stitch

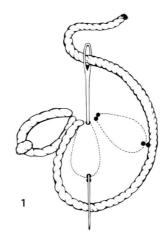

1

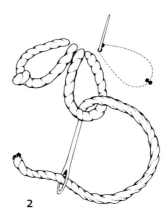

2

Bullion Stitch

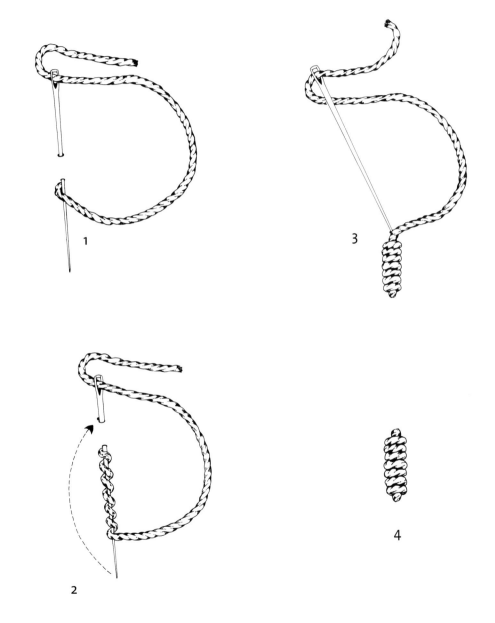

1

2

3

4

Lazy Daisy Bullion Stitch

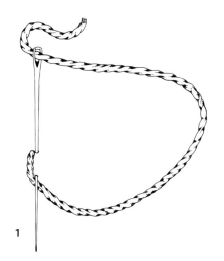

1

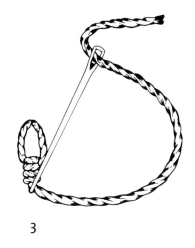

3

2

4

French Knot

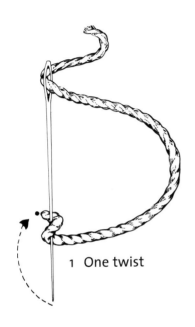

1 **One twist**

Two twists

2

Palestrina Stitch

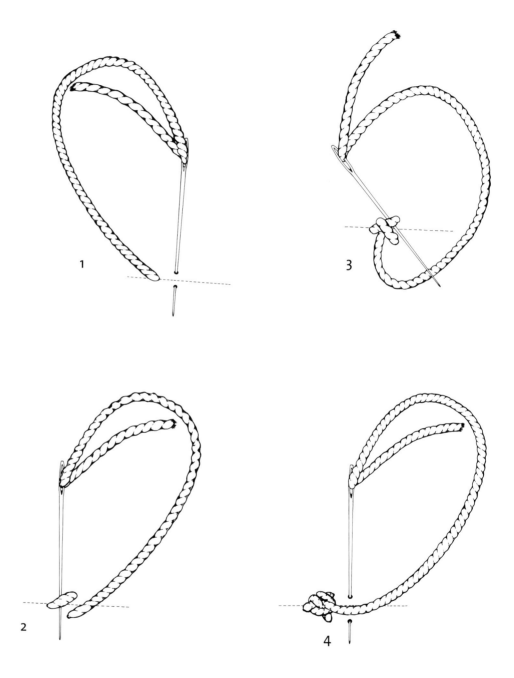

1

2

3

4

Crochet Stitches

The basis of every crochet pattern is the chain stitch—a series of one loop pulled through another loop. This is used to begin most crochet patterns and is the equivalent of casting on in knitting. Once you have mastered this stitch you will be able to work any given pattern. If you are a beginner, use a large hook and fairly thick wool to practise. To begin any piece of work start with a loop on the hook secured with a slip knot. Do the stitches again and again until you are familiar with them and can work quite quickly.

RIGHT-HANDERS

1. Hold the hook in the right hand, usually as if holding a pencil.
2. The left hand holds the work and also controls the wool supply while regulating the tension which is necessary for even work.
3. Arrange the wool around the fingers of the left hand as illustrated to enable control of the wool as needed.

LEFT-HANDERS

Follow the same instructions by reading 'right' as 'left' and vice versa.

It may be helpful to use a mirror to reflect the diagrams in reverse.

SLIP KNOT

Make a loop of wool with the left hand, and holding the hook in the right hand hook another loop through it. Tighten gently and slide the knot up to the hook.

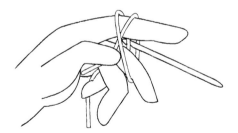

CHAIN STITCH (ch)

1. Holding the wool in the left hand, place the hook—which holds a secured loop—under the thread, and in an anticlockwise movement make a loop on the hook.

2. Draw this loop through the secured loop on the hook to form a new loop.

3. To make a chain simply repeat the process to make as many chain as required.

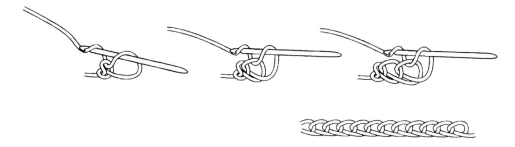

SLIP STITCH (sl st)

With a stitch on the hook, insert the hook into the required stitch of your work, wrap the wool around the hook to form a loop, then draw the loop through the work and the loop on the hook in one movement.

(This stitch is often used to end off work, or to move from one area of work to another).

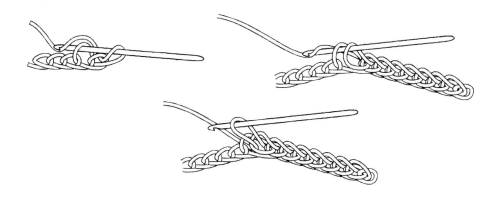

DOUBLE CROCHET (dc)

With a stitch on the hook, insert the hook into the required stitch of the work.

1. Wrap the wool around the hook to form a loop. Draw the loop through the work only.

2. Wrap the wool again to form a loop, and draw the wool through both loops on the hook.

TREBLE (tr)

1. With a stitch on the hook, wrap the wool around the hook to form a loop and insert the hook into the required stitch of the work.

2. Wrap the wool around the hook to form a loop, and draw the loop through the work only.

3. Wrap the wool again to form a loop, and draw the loop through the first two loops.

4. Wrap the wool again and draw the loop through the last two loops on the hook.

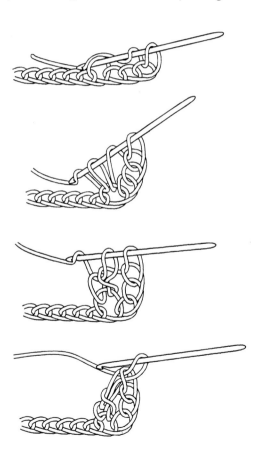

DOUBLE TREBLE (dtr)

1. With a stitch on the hook, wrap the wool twice around the hook to form two loops and insert the hook into the required stitch of the work.

2. Wrap the wool around the hook to form a loop, and draw the loop through the work only.

3. Wrap the wool again to form a loop, and draw the loop through the first two loops.

4. Wrap the wool again and draw the loop through the next two loops on the hook.

5. Wrap the wool again and draw the loop through the last two loops on the hook.

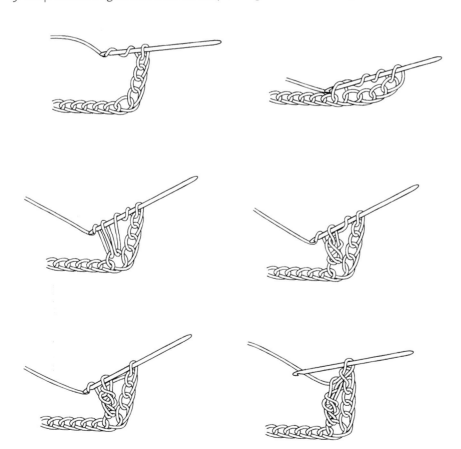

Crochet diagrams by Don Bradford

Thread Conversion Chart for Pansies

DMC SIX STRAND FLOSS		FINCA	APPLETON'S WOOL	SOIE D'ALGER
blanc neige (white)		1000	991B	blanc
154	very dark grape	—	607	5116
155	medium dark blue violet	2699	894	1343
208	very dark lavender	2615	454	1334
209	dark lavender	2606	451	3313
210	medium lavender	2606	885	3334*
211	light lavender	2687	884	3322*
221	very dark shell pink	1996	226	4624
223	light shell pink	1981	754, 755	2932
224	very light shell pink	7806	753	4621
300	very dark mahogany	7656*	767	4215
301	medium mahogany	7740	478	2616
307	lemon	1222	552*	535*
310	black	0007	993	noir
315	med. dark antique mauve	2123	714	4645
316	medium antique mauve	2110*	712	4634
327	dark dark violet	—	455	3315
333	very dark blue violet	2699*	895	1344
340	medium blue violet	2699*	893	1343
341	light blue violet	2732	892	4912
355	dark terracotta	1996	208	616, 2636
356	medium terracotta	7813*	206	4612
370	medium mustard	7318	334, 333	2212
371	mustard	7318, 8320	333	3833
400	dark mahogany	7656	479	4141
444	dark lemon	1227	553	536, 543
445	light lemon	1217	551	2523
471	very light avocado green	4885	543, 354	2124
472	ultra light avocado green	4799	251A	2122, 2123
550	very dark violet	2635*	456	3316
552	medium violet	2627	454	1314
610	dark drab brown	8327	955	4536
725	topaz	1062	554	522

DMC SIX STRAND FLOSS		FINCA	APPLETON'S WOOL	SOIE D'ALGER
726	light topaz	1010*, 1062*	552	522
727	very light topaz	1134*	996	521
734	light olive green	5224*	241	2211
739	ultra very light tan	4000	851	05
741	medium tangerine	1152	556	624
742	light tangerine	1140	555	545
743	medium yellow	1062	473	522
744	pale yellow	1137	472	542
745	light pale yellow	1137	471	2531
746	off white	1211	871	crème
778	very light antique mauve	2098	711	2941
780	ultra very dark topaz	8072	766	4213
782	dark topaz	7155	475	2534
791	very dark cornflower blue	3324*	896	4916
792	dark cornflower blue	—	895	4914
801	dark coffee brown	8080	304	4116
814	dark garnet	2171	759	946
823	dark navy blue	3327*	106	161
829	very dark golden olive	7073	914	526
830	dark golden olive	7066	954	3744
834	very light golden olive	7046	855	2233
838	very dark beige brown	8171	583	4123
839	dark beige brown	8327	186	4115
898	very dark coffee brown	8080	305	4131
902	very dark garnet	2171	149	4625
915	dark plum	2415	805	3026
918	dark red copper	7656*	724	2626
919	red copper	7580*	726	616
920	medium copper	7580	478	2625
937	medium avocado green	4823*	546	2126
938	ultra dark coffee brown	8171	582	4132
939	very dark navy blue	3327	852	163
945	tawny	7936*	708	2911

DMC SIX STRAND FLOSS		FINCA	APPLETON'S WOOL	SOIE D'ALGER
950	light desert sand	7936	202	1011
951	light tawny	7933	705	641
972	deep canary	1232	555	545
973	bright canary	1227	553	534
975	dark golden brown	7656	767	4215
3041	medium antique violet	8620	933	5113
3042	light antique violet	8605	603	5112
3046	medium yellow beige	7225	331	2141
3078	very light golden yellow	1214	841	2121
3346	hunter green	4561	545, 546	2115
3347	medium yellow green	4885	544, 355	2114, 2125
3350	ultra dark dusty rose	2165	757	3025
3362	dark pine green	5075	356	3725
3371	black brown	8083	587	4146
3685	very dark mauve	2246	758	3026
3687	mauve	2240	145	3024
3721	dark shell pink	1996	225	—
3722	medium shell pink	1984	755	—
3726	dark antique mauve	2110	713	4645
3727	light antique mauve	2098	711	1311*
3740	dark antique violet	8620*	605	4635*
3743	very light antique violet	8599	891	3332
3746	dark blue violet	2699	894	1343
3747	very light blue violet	2729	886	4911
3770	very light tawny	8140	877	4241
3772	very dark desert sand	7944	124	4613*
3774	very light desert sand	7933	704	2911
3776	light mahogany	7644	863	2634
3778	light terracotta	7813	205	2633
3802	very dark antique mauve	2123	147	4646
3803	dark mauve	2246	146	3026*
3820	dark straw	1040	473	2533
3823	ultra pale yellow	1128	872	531

DMC SIX STRAND FLOSS	FINCA	APPLETON'S WOOL	SOIE D'ALGER
3834 dark grape	2635*	606	4646
3836 light grape	2098	602	1312
3837 ultra dark lavender	2627	453	1324
3853 dark Autumn gold	7726	557	612
3854 medium Autumn gold	7726	861*	2614
3856 ult vy light mahogany	7720	861	2632
3857 dark rosewood	7656*	127	4615, 4616
DMC blend 937 and 3362	4823	356	2126
* *not good cross match*			

Appendices

DMC size pansy templates

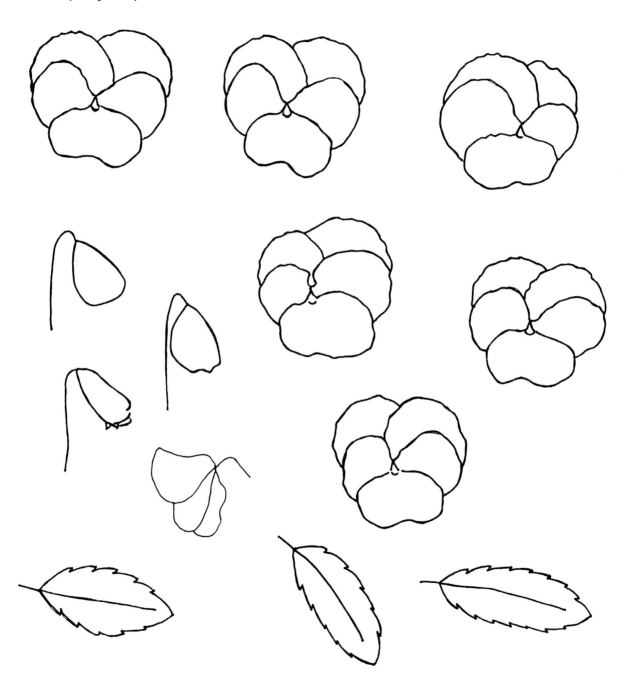

Wool size pansy templates

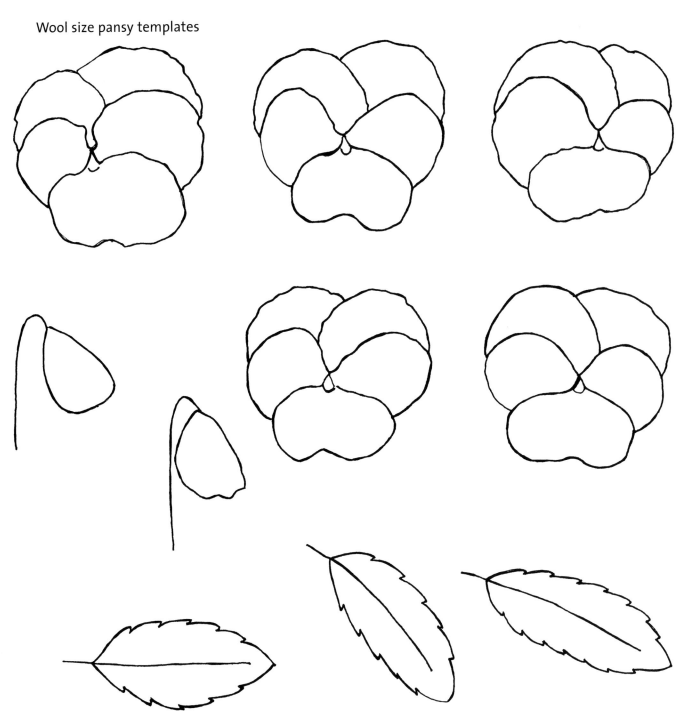

Heartsease templates

1 Small

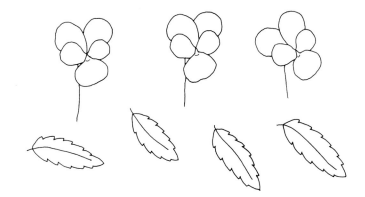

2 Medium

Heartsease templates

3 Large

Heart of Pansies

Cushion Design
This diagram is 85% of actual size
Enlarge diagram by 117%

'Pansies'

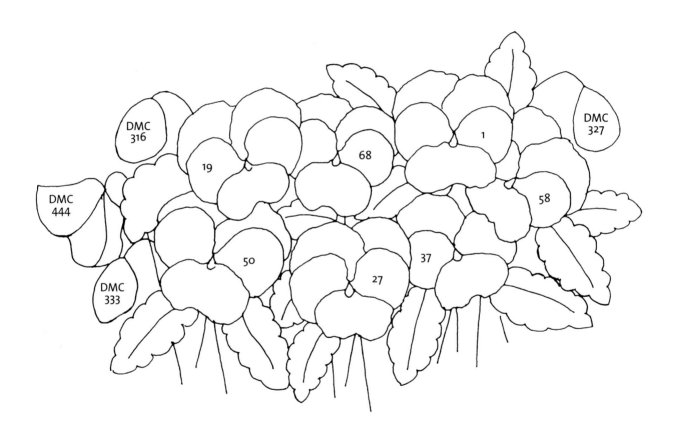

Heartsease Specimen

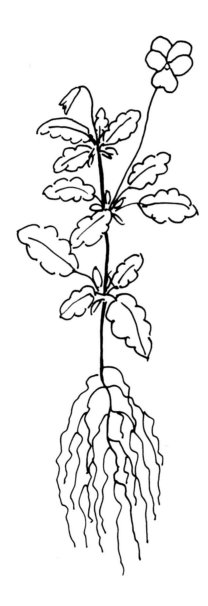

Needlecase

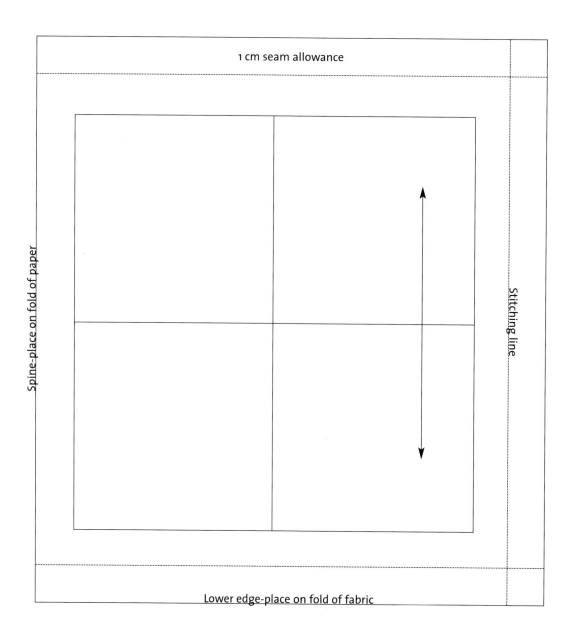

1 cm seam allowance

Spine-place on fold of paper

Stitching line

Lower edge-place on fold of fabric

Spectacle Case

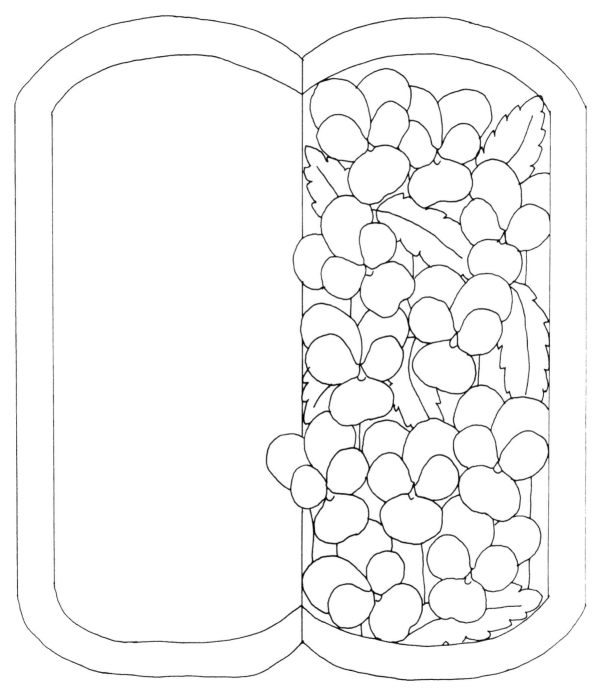

Index